MW01634202

SPOKEN SUCCESS

Understanding The Art Of Public Speaking

ROBERT LITTLE

RELDE Publishing
P.O. Box 21304
Jackson, MS 39289

Library of Congress Control Number: 2001091803

Publisher's Cataloging-in-Publication
(Provided by Quality Books, Inc.)

Little, Robert, 1959-
    Spoken success : understanding the art of public
speaking / by Robert Little. -- 1st ed.
    p. cm.
    ISBN 0-970-18632-0

    1. Public speaking. I. Title.

PN4121.L48 2001   808.5'1
                 QBI21-158

Printed in the United States by:
Morris Publishing
3212 East Highway 30
Kearney, NE 68847
1-800-650-7888

Dedication

I dedicate this work to the memory
of my mother, Lula B. Little, whose teachings
are ever-present in my life today.

Preface

If you have ever wondered why something (public speaking) that's so common and expected, yet can be for many, so horrifying and inhibiting—this book is for you.

My hope is this book will serve as an invaluable resource for your public speaking needs. Keep it handy to serve as your personal desktop reference. I have made an immense effort to address all issues concerning public speaking.

Throughout this book, I have peppered it with questions, comments and experiences that have surfaced during the countless seminars that I have conducted. In doing this, my desire is to create for you, as much as possible, the same experience as if you were participating in one of the sessions.

Additionally, I have included some techniques that are used by speakers that are considered "some of the best" in public speaking. I trust you will find them useful.

For the novice public speaker, in reading this book, you will gain a wealth of knowledge and insight that are sure to reduce your public speaking learning curve.

Acknowledgments

I wish to thank my wife, Lennie, for believing in me. I thank our son, Elliott, for encouraging me in his own way to write this book and showing that he really did understand the importance of daddy getting his book completed.

To my father, Willie Little, for whom I think the greatest compliment is to hear others say, "I emulate you."

Special thanks to Pamela Confer for reviewing and critiquing this book and for her expertise in public relations. I am grateful to Chris Gilmer, Ph.D., acting head of the Department of English at Tougaloo College, for editing the text of this book.

My special thanks to members of Toastmasters International, especially the members of the Capital City Toastmasters Club. Without your candid evaluations and steadfast encouragement, I would not have fully realized the enormity of my deficiencies, nor the magnitude of my growth in public speaking.

Additionally, I wish to express my appreciation to the National Speakers Association and its members for their willingness to share the intricacies of the speaking profession.

Thanks to all of my seminar participants for sharing your experiences and knowing that there has to be a way to transform the butterflies to allies. Finally, thanks to the thousands of audience members who have entrusted me to stand before you as a speaker. I'm truly indebted.

Contents

Chapter 1

Advantages Of Good Public Speaking Skills

Would you like to develop the power to inspire others? Would you like to improve your self-confidence? Would you like to expand your influence in the business, social and political community? Would you like to command more respect from your subordinates, peers, and even your boss?

If you answered "yes" to any of the aforementioned questions; then all you need to do is sharpen your public speaking skills.

If you want to bring success in your life, sharpen your public speaking skills.

If you want others to look to you for leadership, sharpen your public speaking skills.

There is an infinite number of reasons why you should sharpen your public speaking skills. Many times, being a good public speaker with a powerful delivery can achieve better results than strong contents.

Unfortunately, I was 30 years old before I understood the importance and the necessity of good public speaking skills. Even today, I'm still astounded by the many benefits of possessing such skills. It can literally change your life.

Public speaking can help you build your professional and social life. Your ability to articulate thoughts and ideas is critical in every facet of life. Your level of communication causes others to form opinions of you, your product, services, even the company or organization that you represent.

I once heard a story about a training consultant visiting a company executive trying to convince him that his junior managers needed training in public speaking skills. The executive said to the consultant, "What if I train my people and they leave me?" The consultant replied, "What if you don't train them and they stay?" Something to think about, isn't it?

Whether you are an executive or someone who simply has an interest in your continued growth and development, it's never too late to improve your public speaking skills.

Advance Your Career

If you want to advance your career and be a more effective force in the community, it's vital that you hone and sharpen your public speaking skills. It's imperative to be able to turn heads by the elegance of your speech.

People are impressed by those that can articulate well. Most people are more concerned about their physical image—how others see them, particularly their attire. Therefore, they will incur whatever cost that's necessary to fit the bill. Many times, that means buying the most expensive clothes and the best name brands.

Why are people not as concerned about their image as it relates to communicating, particularly public speaking? You should be. It says a lot about who you are. In fact, one can dress in the finest of clothes and open his mouth to speak and the image is immediately blown to bits. That happens all too frequently.

The fortunate aspect of public speaking is everyone

has the ability to become a good public speaker. I find it so unnerving for individuals to take their public speaking skills for granted and make no effort to improve.

I am very much aware of some professionals that are outstanding in their chosen field, but lack the ability to present their ideas in a group setting. I might also add that I know individuals that are outstanding in their chosen field, but lack the ability to present their ideas in a group setting and are constantly passed over for better positions or promotions. Get the message?

Soft Skills Overlooked

Some people are willing to accept the fact that their public speaking skills are holding them back and lack initiative to improve. That amazes me because it's about embracing challenges for your own growth and development. In my opinion, this is due to the focus over the last 20 years on developing technical skills, especially in the technology arena. Soft skills are now being overlooked.

I have long admired individuals that take challenges head-on and I can certainly relate first-hand to the fears of public speaking. I had to take on this challenge some years ago myself. In part, that challenge is why this book is available today.

Employers Pay Attention

I was speaking with an executive in the automotive industry recently. He voiced to me how critical it is to be able to express yourself. He further stated how disheartening it is to see so many people taking communication skills so lightly. Some of his staff had attended one of my seminars.

The analogy he used was a football game. He stated that these individuals may be some of the best players ever, but it doesn't matter if they can't even get on the field to play. You can be a super intelligent individual; however, if you are not able to articulate your intelligence, you will not be given the opportunity to show others what you can do.

This is particularly important, because it proves that you are being judged at all times by your employer.

Critical decisions are being made about you and your career all the time. Employers tend to pay particularly close attention to those who do well at public speaking. Those individuals, with all else being equal, are the ones that move up the ladder of success much faster.

In his arena, they have many technical employees, mostly engineers. He stressed the importance of being able to articulate—in these cases during interviews. One can have an impressive resume, but a good resume can be blown to pieces with a terrible interview.

People with the ability to speak in front of a group in an impressive fashion tend to be regarded as sharp. These people tend to be viewed as leaders. It is no surprise that they tend to be selected for promotions or better positions within organizations.

Take a few seconds to think about the people in your organization. Who are ones that seem to get the promotions? Who are the ones that seem to get the best assignments?

Observe your subordinates; are there at least two individuals that appear to be equal in technical skills?

Which one seems to communicate better with others? Which one would you prefer to represent you at a staff meeting? I'll bet it's the one that communicates best.

I'm also willing to bet that person is also the one that you would be willing to promote ahead of the other one. Guess what? Your boss feels the same as you do.

He or she is interested in promoting the person that communicates best, therefore, representing the organization in a superior fashion. Not to mention, all the added benefits in productivity associated with good communication skills.

Seminars

I have people that have attended my seminars from all walks of life. Some are simply frightened by the idea of speaking before a group of people. Others really don't mind giving presentations, but would prefer not to, if the choice were available.

And, there are those individuals that are always looking to improve their public speaking skills. These are the people who are always looking for a better mousetrap. They are always looking for a better way to make a point or to get an idea across in a new way.

I conduct many seminars during a year. I also attend many seminars during the year as a participant, trying to keep sharp. I have learned the benefits of continuing education.

Public speaking is just that—continuing education. I regard public speaking as a journey, not a destination. You never truly arrive. I have never met a public speaker that couldn't improve.

Even the most prolific speaker can become better. Even Les Brown, one of the greatest motivational speakers today, a man that I idolize for his public speaking skills, can improve.

Selling Yourself

In my seminars, I frequently ask the participants, "How many of you are in sales?" Generally, one or two participants raise their hands. I have found this to be an excellent way to illustrate the need for good public speaking skills. Then, I look at the audience in amazement for a few seconds.

Initially, from their facial expressions, I can easily surmise that they are wondering why I am astonished at so few hands being raised. As the seconds pass, one or two more raise their hands, slowly analyzing my question.

Ultimately, on most occasions up to a third of the participants raise their hands. I sometimes ponder this question for up to five minutes. After a while, I make it known to each participant that we are all in sales.

Everyday of our lives we are selling somebody something. We are selling our children on doing homework. We are selling our spouse on the need for new furniture. We are selling our subordinates on the importance of meeting deadlines. We have to sell our peers in going along with our suggestions.

The participants initially thought I was only referring to the people that were in sales professionally. Unfortunately, most people don't realize that we are all in sales (professionally).

Our public speaking skills play a vital role in determining whether we fail or succeed on a daily basis. We are all selling ideas and recommendations to our spouse, our boss, our employees, our children, our neighbors, etc., all the time. Mainly, though, we are selling ourselves to others.

It is imperative to understand right away that your level of public speaking skills plays an essential role. No matter what your profession may be, your success depends a lot on your speaking skills. Even if you are in a position that doesn't require interaction with others, your speaking skills were instrumental in securing the job.

In this book, I don't promise a lot of false hope. For example, I will not promise you at the completion you will be transformed into a great motivational speaker, but I can assure you that this book provides practical techniques and crucial information essential in becoming a skilled public speaker.

The information provided in this book will aid you in speaking better in a one-on-one conversation, a small staff meeting, a boardroom filled with shareholders, or a coliseum filled with thousands.

Self-Confidence

As you begin to accept more speaking engagements, you'll gain experience and your self-confidence will increase, consequently appreciating the power that effective public speaking commands.

Over time, you'll begin to enjoy public speaking and the tremendous feeling of self-accomplishment that's beyond comparison to anything else.

Remember, the better your public speaking skills, the greater your earning potential. Improving your public speaking is the best investment you'll ever make.

Chapter 2

The Greatest Fear Of All

Why do people fear public speaking? Why are people afraid to speak in front of a group of people? Answer—people are concerned about what others think. Even though people may not openly admit it, they do care what others think of them.

There is concern about how well the speech is going to be received by the audience.

People are concerned about the appropriateness of their speech; what others are saying about their wardrobe, their make-up, their hair, etc. Additionally, people are concerned about whether others think they are competent.

It's important to understand that as you speak, people will look at you. But, as a speaker you want and should expect that.

Expect the audience to stare at you from head to toe. In fact, if they didn't give you their undivided attention, more than likely you would be offended. I would. As the audience is looking at you, they are making decisions about you. Yes, they may very well be asking questions of your attire, competency, etc. There's nothing you can do about that.

Therefore, don't spend valuable time worrying about it. But most important, people are wondering how your presentation will benefit them and how they can relate to you. Sure, some are thinking of who you remind them of and some are thinking about what they don't like about you. Remember, you can do nothing about their thoughts. But, if it's any consolation, some are also thinking positive thoughts of you.

I frequently have had people mention to me during my seminars that I remind them of someone—their pastor, their neighbor, or relatives with positive affirmations and smiling faces.

That's always good. However, I can recall one particular occasion when a woman mentioned to me that I reminded her of her ex-husband. I did not receive any positive feedback from her during the whole day.

Zig Ziglar

Speakers are concerned about things going wrong. This is a real and legitimate fear that shouldn't be ignored. But, it's important not to be consumed by fear. These are fears that we all have.

As speakers, we must always bear in mind what Zig Ziglar, a great motivational speaker, says about fear. He says, "Fear is an acronym for False Evidence Appearing Real." In our minds we create fears for ourselves—fears that never happen.

We can allow our negative minds to come up with some incredible and highly unlikely events. Don't do this to yourself. Think and focus only on positive outcomes. Remember, what you focus on is what ultimately becomes reality.

My point—yes, people are going to think different things about you; yes, they are going to be looking at your wardrobe; yes, you will sometimes remind them of someone they know, favorable and unfavorable people. That goes with the territory.

Nonetheless, your energy and attention should be focused on more important things. More important things like, touching your audience emotionally, stimulating their minds and moving them to action.

Inevitably, there will be times when things will go

wrong; you must never fear these incidents. You can rarely predict them. You can only react to them. One of the best reactions is to acknowledge the incident with humor.

For example, I had a participant in one of my seminars to mention recently that she was reading the introduction of a guest speaker. She read the same line twice. She realized it immediately after completing the sentence for the second time. She simply said, "Hmmm, that sounds familiar" and kept reading the introduction.

The audience laughed and appreciated the manner in which she acknowledged the mistake. She did not panic and yell "excuse me" or "pardon me" in embarrassment. The remark relaxed her and the audience.

Taking Fear Head-On

I find it very ironic that most people experience fear or anxiety associated with public speaking. In knowing and experiencing this fear, it seems that people would simply say, "Everybody experiences fear. Therefore, I will no longer fear public speaking." If only it was this simple—it's not.

I'm reminded of a story that Les Brown tells. There was a man that took the bus to work every day. He would walk about a block and a half to the bus stop. Every afternoon, however, a dog would chase him for half a block.

One day the man got tired of running from the dog. This particular morning he decided to place a brick on the side of the street about the location where the dog always starts to chase him.

His thoughts were, "When this dog starts to chase me this afternoon, I'm going to hit it with the brick."

Sure enough, he got off the bus that afternoon; just like clockwork, the dog was there.

But, this particular afternoon the man was prepared. He wasn't going to run anymore. The dog started barking, the man picked up the brick, saying to the dog, "Come on, I'm ready." The dog continued to approach the man, barking furiously. It got close enough for the man to realize that the dog didn't have any teeth.

Once the man learned this, he threw the brick down and said to the dog "Get away from here." He then realized that the worst that could have happened was the dog would have gummed him to death. This is the approach I emphasize—The fear is legitimate, but just like the man discovered in the story, many of those fears have no teeth in them.

I have always admired great public speakers. I made a conscious decision about eleven years ago to take the fear that I had of public speaking head-on. In the process, I discovered that when you do the thing that you fear to do, you'll gain the power to do it.

In taking head-on the fear that I had of public speaking, I have discovered some things that have been invaluable to me along the way. I will share them with you in this book.

Intimidation

Right out of college, I was employed with an organization that required me to train employees in interviewing people and collecting information from them. Many of these employees had been employed with the agency longer than I had been alive.

Early on, I realized that some employees would use their vast amount of experience and knowledge in an effort to intimidate me. However, I soon discovered that being well-prepared relieved most of the uneasiness I experienced.

Nonetheless, I did a great job at masking the fears that still existed. I always received rave reviews for my training sessions.

I truly enjoyed that aspect of my job and it obviously showed. But, even after receiving rave reviews, I always felt a need to become a better speaker. I wanted to become more comfortable in front of a group. I started a quest for comfort.

Toastmasters International

I had heard of Toastmasters International. I heard that it was an outstanding organization for developing leadership and to sharpen your public speaking skills. I finally attended my first meeting while living in Little Rock, Arkansas.

A friend of mine, Tracy Steele, invited me. He was scheduled to give his first speech, the "Ice Breaker." Full of confidence and well prepared, he gave an excellent presentation. Tracy was an excellent basketball player and his speech focused on how basketball changed his life and afforded him the opportunity to enter college and to go on and do well in life.

He actually used a basketball (as a visual aid) during his presentation. I have seen many "Ice Breakers" since then, none performed as brilliantly as his.

As he was speaking, I was thinking that I should be able to do that. To this day, I'm still not sure whether that was good or bad for me. I say that because if he had done a terrible job, it might have created more fear for me and perhaps I would have never tackled this fear.

On the other hand, in doing the great job that he did, it created a feeling of dichotomy. I wanted to be able to do just as well as he did, but I really didn't feel that I had the skills—more fear. By the way, Tracy became a very visible force in state government and is now a state representative in Arkansas, a position that obviously utilizes his good public speaking skills.

I devised a strategy at the meeting on that day. I had to take this fear head-on. The strategy was to join Toastmasters International and become the greatest public speaker ever. Needless to say, it was short-lived. I never attended another Toastmasters International meeting in Little Rock, Arkansas. The quest was still on, though.

In moving to the Washington, DC area, I still felt a need to improve in the area of public speaking. I heard of a local Toastmasters Club in the area. After a few months, I attended a club meeting.

During this meeting, I was called on to respond to a question for Table Topics. This portion of the program is actually designed for participants to respond to questions extemporaneously.

Now, this beats all. I really wanted to be there, but I was reluctant to go and when asked if I wanted to participate in Table Topics, I agreed. I'm not one to readily walk away from challenges, but I wondered as my name was called if I was in over my head. I answered the question and out of the three of us that spoke, I was selected as winner for the best Table Topic response. I was elated.

So, naturally I attended the next meeting, the next meeting, and the next meeting as a visitor. I became a permanent fixture at their meetings prior to joining. In fact, after my membership was announced at a meeting, some members commented that they thought I was already a member.

Personal Growth

I don't know if winning Table Topics that day sold me on the organization or if after the first meeting I realized it wasn't as painful as I had imagined. Nevertheless, I did join Toastmasters International and in my estimation, it was the best thing I have ever done for my own personal growth and development since completing college.

However, I do sometimes wonder if I would have been as enthusiastic about the organization if I had not won Table Topics at the first meeting.

Overcoming Fear

The first step in overcoming fear is to recognize it for what it is—fear. Fear can rob you of your dreams and direct you down the path of mediocrity. By the same token, however, fear can be the force that can be used to propel you to excellence. Fear in itself is not bad. It's all in how you react to it. I've heard it said that 90% of what we fear never happens and you cannot do anything about the other 10%.

Have you ever had a speaking engagement and you wished that the event was postponed or canceled? Even worse, you would prefer a snowstorm, an earthquake, anything to get out of the speaking engagement. That's fear of public speaking.

10 Worst Fears

Have you ever wondered how the fear of public speaking compares with other fears? Most people have heard that people would rather die than speak in public. I feel that statement is an exaggeration of the truth. I don't know anyone whom, if given the choice would opt for death, rather than speak before a group.

According to David Wallechinsky, Irving Wallace and Amy Wallace authors of the *Book of Lists*, however, fear of speaking before a group ranks higher than the fear of death and is the number one fear of Americans. These are the 10 worst fears of Americans:

10 Worst Fears

1. Speaking before a group
2. Heights
3. Insects, and bugs
4. Financial Problems
5. Deep water
6. Sickness
7. Death
8. Flying
9. Loneliness
10. Dogs

Let's talk about the 10 worst fears and some explanations based on my experience. Starting with number 10:

Fear #10—Dogs: There are some people that fear dogs regardless of their size. It may be a large Doberman or it could very well be a small Chihuahua. It doesn't matter. As long as it's a dog; some people are afraid of them.

My wife is one of those who fears dogs. It can be a cute little dog—to her, it doesn't matter. It's a dog and get it away from her. Our son has been asking for a dog for years. I don't quite know how to tell him that his chances of getting a dog are slim to none. However, my wife has lots of company. There are a lot of people who fear dogs.

Fear #9—Loneliness: People fear being alone. Actually a little solitary time is good for the soul as far as I'm concerned. I believe everybody needs some in order to function properly. Certainly, speakers do.

However, the fear associated with loneliness may have more to do with the time of the loneliness more than anything else.

For example, some elderly people fear loneliness because it could mean spending their golden years alone or in a nursing home. Others grapple with it during certain times of the year, particularly during holidays.

Fear #8—Flying: The fear of flying in an airplane is fairly common. I happen to know quite a few people that consume a lot of alcohol prior to getting on an airplane. The justification that I have heard is simple: They don't feel comfortable flying; therefore, they feel a lot better after a few drinks.

I have flown so much that I very rarely have second thoughts about it anymore.

I was speaking with a group of people recently about the fear of flying and one person made a remark that was quite striking. I mentioned that my fear of flying has basically dissipated, but I do remember my first few flights many years ago when the fear was at its peak.

Nonetheless, I would find comfort in the calmness of other people. I went on to say that sometimes now, however when it gets a bit bumpy, I do become concerned.

One person mentioned that during rough flights, she is mindful of the flight attendants' facial expressions. "If they look worried then I become worried," she remarked.

I have heard people say that they will not get on an airplane, unless they can keep one foot on the ground. The only scenario that I can think of with that happening is not a nice one. Nevertheless, the fear of flying is real.

Fear #7—Death: I was surprised to discover that the fear of death ranked seventh. I thought it would rank higher. But, after further examining the 10 worst fears, it became obvious why it ranks so low.

Death is inevitable. I am going to die. You are going to die and everyone you know is going to die. It's a fact of life. Therefore, there is no reason to walk around fearing it. This is one thing that is beyond your control—so, why fear it.

Fear #6—Sickness: Now, what was interesting about this is people fear sickness more than death. I have heard this and perhaps you have, too. People will say rather than have a prolonged sickness, they would rather go ahead and die. We all have heard of people learning of their fatal illness and opting for immediate death.

Fear #5 - Deep Water: I can relate to this fear. I fear deep water. I am a fisherman. At least, I like to tell people that I am. I have seen television shows showing the great catches on lakes, rivers and oceans.

I have always dreamed about going deep-sea fishing someday, but not soon. Not only do I get seasick, but I fear deep water. I have heard others say that if they can't drink all of the water, they are not going to get in it.

Fear #4—Financial Problems: Most people can relate to this one. No one wants to experience financial problems. Therefore, precautionary measures are taken to avoid them.

Fear #3—Insects and Bugs: Now, I'm an old country boy and I grew up swatting bugs. We didn't have air conditioning in our home when I was a kid. Therefore, in an attempt to cool the house or release some heat from within, we would open the windows.

Various types of insects and bugs would fly in our home. So, it became my responsibility to chase them out or to swat them. So, it's difficult for me to relate to this one, but it's obviously very common.

Fear #2—Heights: I can appreciate this one. I am one of those who fears heights. Whenever I'm climbing up ladders or anything high, I always get the urge to look down. However, I'm told that you should never do that.

Never look down if you are afraid of heights. Looking down causes you to be more frightened. I have also learned that some people have been drawn to jump off high places after focusing on looking down. I think my reason for looking down is to see how far I would fall, if I were to fall.

Fear #1—Speaking before a group: People fear public speaking. Plain and simple—cut and dried. The interesting thing about this, however, is it's a learned fear. People are not born fearing public speaking. We're born with only two fears—The fear of loud sounds and the fear of falling.

Now, what's done with our newborns. In a playing manner, we toss them in the air and allow them to fall. We think that babies love it because of their weird facial expressions. We also clap our hands really loud to see if little ones can turn their heads quickly. They fear loud sounds. Little babies have only two fears and, as adults, we take advantage of both.

We do not have any fears of public speaking when we're born. We began to fear speaking before a group based upon our experiences that we've gained throughout life.

Good News And Bad News

I have good news and bad news about this fear. I'll give you the bad news first. You'll never get over this nervousness or anxiety associated with speaking before a group.

The good news, however, is you don't want to. This nervousness is what you can use to propel your performance from mediocre to excellent.

Learning that *others* feared public speaking really helped me in dealing with my fears of public speaking.

People that I thought were excellent speakers revealed to me that they, too, were nervous. I would ask candid questions of speakers after they delivered, in my opinion, great presentations.

I would ask if they were nervous or felt anxiety prior to or during their presentation. They candidly replied "absolutely." That meant a lot to me. I discovered that if these people could deliver great presentations like that while nervous, then there is hope for me.

Tony Jeary, an international presentation coach, who has trained thousands of people all over the world, says, "The day that I stop feeling nervous is the day I know I'm no longer an effective presenter."

Zig Ziglar says, "Everyone has butterflies in their stomach. The only difference between a pro and an amateur is: the pro has the butterflies in formation."

Most people get very nervous when asked to speak before a group. And many will avoid speaking before a group of people at all cost.

Being nervous is natural and it's normal. A question that I'm asked frequently in my presentation skills seminars is, "How do you make the butterflies go away?" referring to the nervousness or anxiety associated with public speaking. The answer: They don't go away and you really don't want them to.

The adrenaline associated with doing the presentation is that extra boost that can be used to help you make an excellent presentation. You don't want it to go away. Trust me; you don't. Athletes have known and have grown to depend on adrenaline to propel them to the next level.

I have a good friend that is in management with a well known and respected company. He says he never gets nervous before or during a presentation. He constantly tells me this. I always mention to him that it's perfectly normal to experience nervousness. But, he insists, it never happens to him.

Recently, however, he mentioned an occasion when he had to go out of town to his company's headquarters to give a presentation. All of his bosses were there. He said that he was taking medications for an ailment.

While doing his presentation, he started to experience cotton mouth or dry mouth. He became nervous because he was having dry mouth. He refused to say dry mouth was the way he revealed nervousness, that his nervousness caused dry mouth. He said instead that he only got nervous because the dry mouth was occurring.

I did not argue with him. I never argue with people that insist they never get nervous before or during a speech. I have heard that there are two types of speakers: 1) Those who are nervous and 2) Those who are liars.

Even the most experienced speakers become nervous or anxious. It's important to be able to channel the nervousness to work in your favor. That extra energy can work for you, or it can work against you. The decision is yours.

Nervous Energy

Let's try to understand why that nervous energy exists. When it's determined that you must speak before a group of people, your body reacts as if you are in a threatening situation. Now, how soon our bodies react depends on the person and situation.

Some people are informed of a speaking engagement weeks or months ahead of time and their bodies will start to react right away. Some people start to feel jitters just days before the event.

On the other hand, there are others who become nervous only on the day of the event or just minutes before having to speak. It varies. I know some people that have many sleepless nights, counting down to the day of the speech.

Fight Or Flight

Nonetheless, your body's natural reaction in a threatening situation is "fight or flight." Those are natural reactions. Typically, when we are giving presentations, we don't have a reason to fight anyone.

You may not care to give the presentation, your boss or someone might insist that you do, but still this is no reason to fight.

Flight is the other alternative. I have seen some people take advantage of this one. They simply decide that they can't do it. Some refuse to take the stage during the function; there are others that will cancel days before the event.

Adrenaline Begins To Pump

As a speaker, your desire is to do good. Therefore, fight and flight are ruled out. However, when that happens your body starts to react in strange ways. Your blood pressures rises. Your heart rate increases. Sometimes, you start to perspire. Your hands may even start to shake or tremble. Sometimes, even your knees may start to shake or you get noodle knees, as it has been called. Adrenaline begins to pump. All sorts of things start to happen.

We become nervous because we all have a desire to do our very best. If we really didn't care about the presentation, nervousness would not be a problem.

Many times, there is a lot at stake, particularly when it's important that you impress someone. We want to look good for the boss, for our family and for ourselves. People are accustomed to doing their best, therefore, nervousness exists.

Ways Nervousness Is Revealed

Nervousness shows itself in many ways. It's important to know and to understand that different people have different ways of revealing nervousness.

There is no correlation between how well one can speak in public and his or her IQ. As a matter of fact, I have seen some truly intelligent individuals bomb during presentations, just as I have seen some people that weren't as sharp do just as badly. Good public speaking skills can be acquired by all who are interested in developing them, regardless of IQ.

It's important to learn to laugh at mistakes that you make. In fact, it has been said, "Laugh at yourself and beat everybody else to the punch." Learn to loosen up. People many times have unrealistic expectations in public speaking. They expect perfection and when that doesn't occur, they feel the entire speech was a disaster.

The first thing you should do in dealing with nervousness is to acknowledge it. Never deny it. Now, I don't mean you should acknowledge it to your audience. You should never do that.

Unfortunately, it's done frequently. Speakers stand before a group and the first thing they will say is, "I'm really nervous, so you all bear with me." Never do this for two reasons:

1) If you are going to speak, be prepared to give the audience the best that you have, even if you discovered a few minutes prior to the presentation that you were going to speak. You should not offer an excuse with the intentions of deflating the audiences expectations of you. 2) Your nervousness is never as apparent to the audience as you think. When you announce

that you are nervous, then the audience starts to look for signs of nervousness. It's akin to what I heard sometime ago about wearing dark colored pants and wetting in them; if you don't mention it, chances are no one will know.

Listed below are several ways that speakers reveal their nervousness:

Shaking And Excessive Movement

Some people literally shake or tremble while giving a presentation. Usually it's their hands, but it can sometimes be their arms, legs, or their entire body. People that experience these symptoms should avoid holding objects in their hands, particularly paper.

Even if you decide to hold the paper behind your back, the shaking can still create sound, not to mention the fact that it does not look professional.

And never, I repeat never, try to point out something with a pointer on an overhead projector with the shaking hand. The nervousness is magnified tremendously. I even suggest that you not point it out on the screen, even though the effects are reduced.

If there are situations when you know you will need paper for a specific reason, make sure there is a lectern, podium, or a table nearby to rest your papers on.

It's never a good idea to hold anything for the duration of your speech. I use a music stand in most of my seminars, rather than a lectern or podium. I have found this to be extremely helpful for a number of reasons: 1) It's very portable; 2) I can adjust it fairly easily and quickly; 3) It does not create a barrier between me and the audience.

Even though I do not recommend that anyone speak with his or her hands in their pockets, I would rather see that than shaky hands. The best alternative is to hold temporarily to the lectern or podium until you stop shaking. Once the shaking stops, let go. You need your hands free for gestures.

People that move excessively tend to create a major problem for the audience—it wears them out. Don't misunderstand me. Moving is good. You must always incorporate a certain amount of platform movement into your presentation. But you can do too much of it.

I will discuss the details of platform movements in chapter eight. However, excessive movers like to pace furiously, usually back and forth sometimes from side-to-side. Now, this is an excellent way to use up all of that excess energy. However, it can create a huge distraction from an otherwise good presentation.

I have a friend that is now a prominent attorney. He started his practice in a small, southern town. He said that he knew it was important to make himself known to the community (prospective clients). People would frequently ask him to speak at events in the area.

He always accepted every invitation, even though he felt he was a terrible speaker. That was the only way he could build his business. It was a cheap, yet very effective way of advertising. He mentioned that he would be so nervous that his knees would start to shake and the only thing that saved him was he did not dare move away from the podium while the episodes were occurring.

He wanted to know if that was what he should have done. He did exactly what I would have recommended in staying behind the podium. He knew that he was extremely nervous. There was no need to tell the world.

I always advise clients if they are extremely nervous not to verbalize it to the audience. Only you, the speaker, has to know.

If you experience symptoms such as my friend, the attorney, stay behind the lectern or podium until the episode subsides. Believe me. It will subside. They always do. At the time it may seem like eternity, but it will ultimately subside.

However, when the episodes subside, it's important for you to get out in front so that the lectern or podium will not create a barrier for you and your audience. This, of course, is dependent on whether you will be tied to the lectern or podium because of a microphone.

Loss Of Thoughts

This is embarrassing, I know. Believe me, I know. This can happen at any point during you presentation, but is most embarrassing and can be most devastating at the beginning. It's hard to get going again after it happens. However, you must not dwell on it in order to get back on track.

I have seen people forget their address, phone number, children's names and even their own name. Why is something that is so necessary sometimes so difficult?

Roscoe Drummonds says this: "The mind is a wonderful thing, it starts working the minute you are born and never stops until you get up to speak in public." A true statement.

My father, who I think is a wonderful public speaker, frequently says that when he stands up to speak, his mind sits down. This is typically the opening line of his speeches. It's always a winner with the audience. If this should happen to you, I have two recommendations:

1) Acknowledge that you have gone blank. You can simply say, "I just lost my train of thought" with a smile on your face, which will draw smiles and laughter from the audience. The reason being, it has happened to everyone in the room at some point in time. They can relate and appreciate the honesty.

Also, it shows that you are human. Remember, whenever you can draw laughter from the audience, you are gaining acceptance. Laughter allows you to relax a bit and carry on.

2) Digress while trying to regain your thoughts. However, you must be careful when using this technique. Mainly, because you risk the possibility of losing your audience. They may start to wonder what the information you are now sharing has to do with the original topic.

Have you ever wondered if experienced or seasoned speakers ever lost their train of thought? Is a blue sky blue? However, most experienced speakers have their own way of "filling in" without the audience being aware.

One technique is to simply move along to the next information that you had planned to share with your audience. Remember, only you know your speech. However, if it is critical information that is vital in making a point later, you had better think of a way to include it.

You can always throw in a bit of humor, for example, "I forgot what I was going to say." Then you can say, "I have a great memory. It's just short." Or you can simply say "I'm having a senior moment, here." This will certainly draw laughter from the audience.

Additionally, you can repeat the previous statement or mention the theme or title of your speech again. Cleverly weave it in. The audience will never know that you are stalling for time in an effort to recall your presentation. By doing this, it will buy you a few seconds. That is all the time you need.

Another technique is to say "I wonder...", while placing your pointer finger to your temple or placing your chin in your hand.

It's critical that you exhibit the proper body language while utilizing this technique, which should be that of a person in deep thought. Precisely, you are in deep thought. Just that you are trying to think of your presentation, but want your audience to think you are coming up with a fresh, new idea.

It's important, however, that you have a very pleasant smile on your face when using these lines, because you must remember, your audience will always mirror you.

If you look out at the audience with a terrified facial expression, they are going to look at you the same way. On the other hand, if you look out at them with a smile on your face, they are going to smile back at you.

Sweatin' Bullets

I don't mean perspiring. I mean sweatin'. It might be in the form of little beads on your forehead or it may come like a drenching rain. Sweaters also tend to have sweaty palms.

Good news for those who have the little beads of sweat—depending on the distance between you and the audience, they may not be able to see it. But, it begins to be a problem when the little beads continue to form and turn into big beads and start to roll off the tip of your nose. Then, something has to be done.

Whether you have little beads or big beads, it's perfectly okay to have a handkerchief at your disposal to wipe off the perspiration as it becomes uncomfortable or noticeable. Be careful in using Kleenex or napkins since they may leave little particles on your face.

I must add this, however, a lot of dynamic speakers sweat while speaking. The perspiration has little to do with nervousness, but has more to do with the amount of adrenaline and passion the speaker has toward the subject matter.

Some people actually perspire due to their physical movements in giving a speech. Therefore, sweating is not always an indication of nervousness.

In my church, for example, our pastor is a great speaker and we have grown to expect him to sweat. So, if he completes a sermon without sweating, we look over at a neighbor and say, "He really didn't preach today, did he?"

Tongue Twisters & Speedsters

An example of this is not being able to pronounce words that you know and have been saying for years, but due to nervousness you can't get them out. This has happened to most people.

I always ask participants in my seminars to say tongue twisters and speedsters three times really fast. Try it. Say "tongue twisters and speedsters" three times really fast. It's very difficult to do.

One of the most common ways to react to this one is to exaggerate the incident by saying, "Bloobbbbb, gee, I can't talk today." To respond to it humorously, you can say, "I hope you understood that, because I sure didn't." Usually that will get smiles and laughter from the audience.

Now, the speedsters are people whose rate of speech increases as they become nervous. The more nervous they get, the faster they speak. Don't think for one minute they are going to slow down, because they're not. They are going to say what they have to say, so they can sit. If you didn't understand them, it's your problem. Their goal is to make it back to their seats as quickly as possible.

I have trained countless people in public speaking skills and I have never had anyone to come to me following a seminar and say, "I usually slow down when I get nervous." No, that doesn't happen.

People tend to speed up when nervous. Once you recognize this as a problem, you have done half the work. The best way to remedy this problem is to solicit the help of someone else.

Most people don't realize it when they are speaking too fast. Some do, but most don't. The best way to correct this problem is to have someone sitting in the audience that you can make eye contact with to give you signals to indicate to you that your rate of speech should be slowed. It is quite difficult to correct this problem on your own.

Dry Mouth

Dry mouth or cotton mouth can be very uncomfortable and a distraction to your audience. When experiencing dry mouth, you need liquid.

To have my seminar participants to master this, I share an exercise with them that I learned sometime ago. Here is the exercise we do. See if it works for you. Visualize this: I have in my hand a big, yellow lemon. I place the lemon on the table and cut it in half. As I cut the lemon, the juices gush out all over my fingers and the table.

Did this create additional juices in your mouth? It usually does for most people. In my seminars I have them to close their eyes and follow along with me as I talk them through it.

This is a technique that can be employed over time. However, it is a bit much to expect an inexperienced speaker to be able to visualize this while giving a presentation.

The best solution for people with cotton mouth is to sip water until the dryness goes away. Drinking while speaking can be a distraction; however, in this case, it is the lesser of the two evils.

This is the only time that I would ever recommend drinking during a presentation. I've even seen people drink water, soda, iced tea or coffee in mid-sentence. They make drinking a part of their presentation. This can be an extreme form of distraction. If you must drink due to dry mouth, drink water.

Warm water is best. So instead of asking for coffee, ask for warm water, if you are speaking at a luncheon or banquet. Warm lemon water is even better. By the way, I never advise, drinking alcohol prior to or during a presentation.

Fixers

These are the people that insist on fixing the microphone. I have seen these people and I'm sure you have, too. Every other sentence, they must adjust the microphone. They continue to adjust it until one of two things happens—They accidentally cut the microphone off or they knock it down. Then they are satisfied.

They will many times make a remark like "Oops, what happened?" As if they really don't know. However, they move onto toying with their notes or playing with the paper clip on their notes. It does not matter what it is they are fixing, just as long as they fix something. They must do something with their hands.

To remedy this problem, I advise clients to hold on to the lectern or podium. People that are aware of this distraction many times believe the only alternative is to put their hands in their pockets.

That is an alternative, but one that you should employ only after you try holding on to the lectern. This again is an evil, but the lesser of the two. Otherwise, your hands should be left free for gestures.

Scratchers And Pickers

These people feel compelled to scratch body parts. They may start with their hands, then move to their arms. Sometimes, they will start with their nose or chin, but ultimately end up scratching their head or forehead. They are unconsciously scratching during their presentation.

I once had a supervisor that would always scratch during presentations. He never felt comfortable in talking with the staff. He had a routine of first scratching his nose, then his head (all in one pass). He would do it about every three to four minutes. After a while, it became a terrible distraction.

In fact, it became such a distraction that people started to time the frequency. Obviously, no one was focusing on his presentation, just his bad habits. It finally got to the point where employees would make comments about it saying, "I think he has lice."

The pickers are those that start to pick at things like their fingernails or nose. I must also include in this category the ear diggers, too.

Others

This category includes people that seem to experience shortness of breath while speaking. Now, breathing is not something that we think about. It just happens. However, nervousness does affect some people's breathing patterns. This creates a tremendous amount of frustration and discomfort.

I have seen this affect people's speaking voice for up to three to four minutes into their presentation. After a while, they get it under control. The best thing to do in those situations is to pause for about a second and take a deep breath. It may seem like a minute to you in taking this deep breath, but generally the job can be done in two to three seconds. That allows you to continue with your presentation while breathing normally.

A cracky or quivering voice is a symptom that is experienced by some. This is particularly embarrassing when the first words uttered are with a cracky voice. I have seen this done and speakers' reactions vary.

Typically their facial expressions are all the same— where did that come from? The best remedy for this is to breathe deeply as you are being introduced and sip water prior to going to the lectern or podium. Additional information concerning ways to reduce nervousness and preparation techniques will be shared in the next two chapters.

Prepare

As mentioned at the beginning of the chapter, nervousness is revealed in a number of ways. People have their own ways of revealing nervousness. What's most important is knowing your way of revealing nervousness—then prepare for it.

Even though, this sounds to be an easy remedy to the problem, I am stunned as to how few people have figured out how to deal with it. Again, the key to being able to effectively deal with your way of revealing nervousness is to *prepare* for it.

Prepare for it just as you look out and prepare for a rainy day. Even if it doesn't rain, there is peace of mind in knowing you are ready, regardless.

Generally, people know beforehand the ways they reveal nervousness. It is most often known from past experiences. You have to view this in its positive light. Now that you know, take advantage of this knowledge and take the proper precautionary measures. Be ready to deal with the situation before it happens.

For instance, if you know you get cotton mouth, make arrangements to have water to sip. If you know you are a sweater, have a handkerchief ready. Being prepared to deal with your nervousness actually reduces it.

Amazing, isn't it? Regardless of your form of nervousness, it is just your body's way of letting you know that you have a tremendous task ahead of you and you have the resources to excel.

I have had people to come to me after seminars and say, "I have experienced all of the symptoms of nervousness we discussed on today." That's perfectly okay. Even if you have multiple ways of revealing nervousness, you can still be an outstanding speaker.

Just like every speaker brings to the table his natural speaking skills, which vary from person to person, each person has his own way of revealing nervousness.

During my seminars, I have had people to ask the question, "Why do people do this to themselves? Why are they willing to go through agony and great pains to speak before a group of people?"

There are varying reasons—some people do it because their jobs require them to. Others do it because they are in leadership positions in their community, their church, or their organizations. What truly impresses me is when a person says, "I had to do it, because I'm determined to take this fear head-on for my own personal growth and development." I truly think this is the reason why you are reading this book.

I believe that the person that brings the most nervousness to the table has the potential to become the best speaker.

I believe this primarily because they have the most energy for use and when they master the skills of harnessing that energy and focusing it in the right direction, they can be awesome. They must learn that the aim is not to make the butterflies go away, but to have them to fly in formation.

"Yeah, right," you might say. Well, even I have to admit that it's easier said than done. But, we will discuss some ways that will make you appear as if you are as cool as a cucumber. As I have heard Les Brown say, "Act the way you want to be and soon you'll be the way you act."

Chapter 3

Techniques To Reduce Nervousness

Nervousness or anxiety is experienced by the most seasoned speakers. Being nervous in speaking before a group is normal. From the previous chapter, we know that nervousness is one of the key ingredients for a great presentation.

However, wouldn't it be nice if there were a knob to turn, a button to punch, or some way to adjust the amount of nervousness to get the best results—just enough to be outstanding?

For example, just as you may use a microwave oven to pop popcorn—most of the kernels pop without burning it, when you push the preset popcorn button.

Even consider cooking recipes for meat dishes, depending on the weight you can set the oven to a certain temperature and expect it to turn out okay at the recommended time. Unfortunately, it doesn't work that way with nervousness and public speaking.

However, there are techniques that can be used to reduce nervousness. If I told you these techniques would eliminate nervousness, I would be lying. But, most important, I would be suggesting removing a necessity for good public speaking.

Eight Simple Techniques To Reduce Nervousness

Practice, Practice, Practice
Prepare To Cheat
Focus On Your Audience
Memorize The Opening And Closing
Use Positive Self-Talk
Visualize Success
Arrive Early
Breathe Deeply

Figure 3.1 Eight Simple Techniques To Reduce Nervousness

Practice, Practice, Practice

I'm reminded of a story I heard about a lady going to perform at Carnegie Hall. She got lost on the way. She stopped to ask a gentleman on the street for directions. She said, "Excuse me sir, how do I get to Carnegie Hall?" The man replied, "Practice, practice, practice." It's important to practice your speech.

It has been suggested that you can reduce your nervousness or fear by 75 percent by simply being prepared. Practice is one thing that will help you more than anything else. It is amazing how it increases your level of comfort.

In my seminars, the participants in an over-whelming majority always indicate that not being prepared is the number one reason for experiencing excessive nervousness.

When I mean practice, I mean practice "effectively." Not just simply preparing your presentation and reading over it a few times and then saying, "Yes, I'm ready." That is not practicing effectively. Much more is required for effective practice. I will discuss effective practicing techniques later in chapter four.

Prepare To Cheat

Do you remember back in middle school when there were some students that attempted to cheat on tests? These students were exploring options of passing tests by means other than studying. They would be very meticulous and creative in their escapades.

Just like them, you should take painstaking efforts to ensure your success. This obviously becomes more of a factor in delivering a speech that you want your audience to believe that you are delivering without notes of any type.

Prepare to cheat. That simply means make notes in strategic locations that will assist you in making your presentation.

Do not write out entire sentences to assist you. Your notes should be keywords and phrases that will trigger a thought or idea when you see them.

There was a situation that occurred to me recently which, in my opinion, provided the perfect situation for this technique even though it was a one-on-one conversation.

A woman visited my office attempting to sell insurance. She obviously had not been employed with the company for very long. She was not very familiar with the company's various insurance packages. She was having difficulty thinking of her lines as part of her sales pitch, as well.

She was struggling. It was obvious to me and I thought I would do her a favor in making her aware of it.

I said, "Mam, I can tell you are fairly new at this. May I make a suggestion to you?" She was holding a folder in her arms as if she were cradling a baby. I said, "The way that you are holding your folder allows you the perfect opportunity to make notes to yourself as you are making your sales calls.

"The only thing you need to do is to write key words and phases on your folder to remind you of certain points. This will allow you to express yourself in a much more comfortable fashion—subsequently, making more sales.

"No one ever has to know that the notes are there. You can casually glance down at them as you speak. But, even if others were to see them, they wouldn't mean anything to them."

I went on to explain to her that it would be an excellent way to become more at ease.

Then, I invited her to attend one of my seminars. I couldn't envision her being successful in sales without a dramatic improvement. She thanked me for the suggestion. I truly believe that she was grateful.

By the way, she attended one of my seminars. I have seen her on a number of occasions since then. She is always thanking me for the candid words and the help that I provided.

In using key words and phrases, you are the only person that would know what they mean. The key words and phases are there to assist you. It doesn't matter where you make the notes; what's important is having them strategically located and knowing what they mean.

Therefore, don't be so conservative in writing them that you don't understand what they mean. On the other hand, don't make so many that when you glance down at them, you are overwhelmed and confused by the massive quantity.

It's also important that your print is large enough for you to glance without having to view them closely. I suggest 15 to 20 point fonts.

I have even seen people make notes in the palms of their hands. However, you must be mindful of this if you are going to be using open-palm gestures. People will obviously see your notes.

Additionally, if you tend to have sweaty palms during your presentations, obviously you don't want to use this technique. When you view them, you'll only have a handful of ink.

By the way, the phrase "Off the cuff" was coined back in the early 1920's. People would make notes on the cuff of their sleeves for them to view while giving their speeches. I wouldn't necessarily suggest this method, unless you want a hefty laundry bill.

Focus On Your Audience

Focus on your audience, not yourself. Remember, your audience wants you to do well. Make them proud of you. Make them pleased that they attended the event.

Let me share some examples with you. Have you ever gone to a banquet and the speaker accidentally knocked over a glass of water or knocked the microphone down? Didn't you feel bad for that person? You were embarrassed for him, weren't you?

Or better yet, have you ever gone to a circus and seen a high-wire act being performed? You're sitting at the edge of your seat and finally, they complete the act. You breathe a sigh of relief, don't you?

It's because you want them to do well, especially if you paid money to see them. You are really pulling for that individual. Well, guess what? Your audience feels the same way about you. They want you to do well. They have come to see you do well. It's imperative that as a speaker, you always bear this in mind.

Memorize The Opening And The Closing

Memorize the opening and the closing. Depending on the purpose of your speech, you should memorize all of it. However, if it's 30 minutes, 45 minutes or an hour, you may consider using notes.

Have you ever had a salesperson to come to your door with a memorized sales pitch? It sounded like a recording. If you should have to interrupt for some reason or another. You can tell they have to try to remember where they left off.

Or, if you have ever received a phone call from a telemarketer, the speeches are memorized and sound as such. Even worse, have you ever received a phone call from a recorded telemarketer? If you have experienced any of these, you remember what kind of lasting impact it had on you. As a speaker, you should avoid sounding like a tape recorder. However, it's imperative that the opening and closing are memorized. When you take the lectern or podium, you are the focus of attention.

All of the attention is on you. When the attention is focused on you, there is just one chance to make a good first impression. This is it. And, this is also the time when you experience nervousness the most—the first two to three minutes of your presentation.

If you have your opening memorized, you'll do well. Your opening comes right out. Obviously, this is not the time to try to think of an opener. This is not the time to ad-lib.

You must grab the audience's attention right away. If you lose them at the opening, you will be fighting an uphill battle throughout your entire presentation. It's imperative to remember that your audience will give you two to three minutes to make an impression—good or bad. They are going to make critical decisions about you in that short period of time.

The close. This is your destination. You have arrived. This is your chance to seal the deal—to tie things together, to have them to see things your way.

Here's your opportunity to have them leaving the event saying, "Wow, what a speaker!" This is the time for your call to action. They will remember best what they hear last. Don't blow it. This is no time to hem-haw around. Memorize it.

Use Positive Self-Talk

It's perfectly okay to pump yourself up. Use positive self-talk or affirmation. In fact, it's critical that you do so. Tell yourself that you are going to do well and you will.

Have there ever been situations when you told yourself that you're going to mess something up? "I'm going to mess up! I'm going to mess up! I know I am." And sure enough, you messed up.

Learn to use affirmations or positive self-talk to pump yourself up. It's very effective. Remember, what you focus on will become reality.

Where I'm from it's said that if you talk to yourself you are crazy. Maybe you have heard that, too. Well, I tend to think of it as crazy like a fox. Crazy like a fox because it is a wise thing to do. You have to.

I've also heard some people say that talking to yourself sometimes is the only way to have an intelligent conversation. Well, so much for that.

Positive self-talk is necessary. It's important to tell yourself that you are going to do well. If you tell yourself that you are going to do well, you will.

On the other hand, if you tell yourself that you are going to fail. You know what? You usually will. So, pump yourself up. Positive self-talk is critical.

I frequently say to myself, "I'm the greatest speaker in the world." I repeat it over and over again. "I'm the greatest speaker in the world. I'm the greatest speaker in the world. I'm the greatest speaker in the world." It's important to feel good about your speaking skills.

Special Note: When I competed in speaking contests, I always prayed before competing. I never prayed to win, only to do well. I'm proud to say I have won many speaking contests. My prayers were always answered. Praying brought me a great deal of comfort. By the way, I still use this technique today, before and after every speaking occasion.

Visualize Success

Visualize success before you make it happen. After pumping yourself up, let your imagination run wild. See yourself delivering a dynamic opening just as you practiced it. Picture yourself delivering the body of your speech with main points being executed superbly.

Envision the ending being very powerful, moving your audience to action. See yourself getting a standing ovation after your speech. See the audience cheering, screaming for you before it happens. Then that becomes your goal. If you can see this in your mind's eye, then you can make it a reality. See it happening and then go make it happen.

Arrive Early

As a general rule, you should arrive well in advance of your presentation. I know speakers that make it their business to arrive an hour prior to their presentation. How far in advance depends on the situation.

If you have equipment that must be tested, or if someone else is setting the room up for you, it's a no-brainer; you have to be there well in advance. It may be fifteen or twenty minutes early for a function in your office or it may be two hours for a formal engagement with many guests.

However, it's important to arrive early. This allows a number of things to occur. First, it allows you to put the host or meeting planner at ease. If you have ever been responsible for a speaker, you can relate to the frustration that can be caused by a speaker being tardy.

I can't begin to tell you how terrible it can be when the speaker arrives late or at the last minute. Additionally, being early allows you time to adequately prepare and to become comfortable. Arriving late only puts additional pressure on you.

Find A Secluded Area

After you have arrived early and have checked-in with the host or meeting planner, do the following:

Find a secluded area. It may very well be the men's room, the ladies' room, or a nearby vacant room. You may need to go back to your car. I have had to do this on a number of occasions. Seek privacy somewhere.

The men's room or ladies' room may not provide the type of isolation that's required. However, it can be used as a last resort. It would be to your benefit to scan the stalls for feet, prior to doing the exercises for loosening up. Otherwise, people will view you strangely and scramble to vacate the restroom.

After you have found a private place, you should do the following three things:

1. Practice your opening again, again and again.

It's important that you practice as many times as necessary so that you will feel comfortable. There is no magic number for the amount of practice, just that you should do it over and over and over until you feel extremely comfortable.

2. Check your appearance.

Check yourself out. Look in the mirror. Check your face, your hair, your wardrobe. Check your teeth, making sure there is no lettuce or meat caught between them, particularly if you've just finished a meal.

An associate told me of an event that recently happened to him. He was conducting a full-day seminar and broke for lunch. He failed to check himself out after eating lunch. He conducted the entire afternoon session with a sesame seed on the bottom of his lip. No one bothered telling him. He noticed it at the conclusion of the session. People are embarrassed to tell you about things like that. Therefore, you can only rely on yourself or perhaps close friends.

Ladies check your lipstick. Men should check your necktie and fly. Yes, your fly—your zipper.

I attended a conference a few years ago and there were several speakers. As one of the speakers was introduced, he walked to the podium and the audience started to laugh. The first thing that he did was to see if his fly was unzipped.

In his mind, the only thing they could be laughing at would be his fly being open. So, he looked down to check it. The crowd roared.

In actuality, one of the dais guests was making a motion with his hands that caused the audience to laugh. It had nothing to do whatsoever with the speaker. At least, not until he checked his fly. So, check yourself out.

A lot is at stake. When you know you're looking good you feel better about yourself. When you feel better about yourself, you perform much better.

3. Exercise.

When I say exercise, I don't mean jumping jacks or push-ups. Although, there are some people that like to do real physical exercises prior to their presentation. I might add that this is certainly a very effective way to use up excess energy.

However, the type of exercise that I'm referring to has to do with relaxing the shoulders, neck, mouth and tongue.

Generally when you have to speak your shoulders are elevated somewhat higher than usual due to the anxiety. They tend to stiffen up. The best thing to do is to rotate the shoulders. In fact, try it right now as you read this book. Rotate them in a circular motion. Do it about five times.

Now after you're done, move to your neck. Rotate your neck in a circular motion for about five times. You may continue for even longer if you so desire. This feels good even when you're not about to speak.

Now to loosen up your mouth and tongue, say "Whoa Nellie, Whoa Nellie, Whoa Nellie, Whoa Nellie, Whoa Nellie." Now, for those of you whom don't care for the Whoa Nellie, there is an alternative. Recite the vowels in an exaggerated fashion. Do them now "A-E-I-O-U." Again, "A-E-I-O-U." And, now for a final time, "A-E-I-O-U."

I'm sure you now understand why this must be done in a secluded area.

Sometimes, I will do this with youth and I'll ask them to pucker up as if they are about to kiss grandma. I will then say, "Remember, she dips snuff." If only you could imagine their facial expressions. Nonetheless, loosening up your mouth, lips and tongue are critical for good enunciation during your presentation.

Meet And Greet

After you have done all that is necessary to deliver a great presentation, don't stay in seclusion. If you stay in the secluded room thinking about your presentation, it will only serve to undermine all of the work that was just done.

You must now go out and meet and greet your audience. Introduce yourself to people. Find out who they are. You will find that as you interact with people, they will tell you about themselves, their families and many will give you more information than you really want.

What is most important about this is you will have the opportunity to make new friends. This also allows you the opportunity to get their names, professions and experiences that you can weave into your presentation.

When you mention someone's name or experience in your presentation, it immediately establishes a bond between you, that person and the entire audience. In doing so, look at the individual as you mention his or her name and experience and notice how that person beams.

Just as important, as you interact with others, you are not focusing on giving a speech, you are meeting people. And, when you are giving your presentation you are not talking to a room full of strangers, you are speaking to your new friends. It certainly improves your confidence as you give your presentation.

If you are unable to visit with the audience due to the type of function or because of a stage, involve yourself in conversations with people around you. This could be the dais guests, program moderator or others. It's important that you focus on something other than your presentation.

Another reason for early arrival is to take the time to get to know the room in which you will be speaking. Walk around the room. Visit each corner. Sit in various seats throughout the room. This gives you the opportunity to see how others will view you.

Additionally, if you find that certain areas of the stage or platform cause difficulty for people to see you, then you should avoid those locations while moving about on the stage. You would only have the opportunity to do this by getting to know the room.

It is no secret that sports teams seem to win most of their games at home. This is because they are familiar with the home location. They feel more comfortable because of the familiarity with the location.

Breathe Deeply

Being nervous is only natural in public speaking. However, this nervousness can cause shallow breathing. This practice can be done at anytime when you start to experience anxiety or nervousness.

It is critical, though, to always breathe deeply as you are being introduced and continue it until you utter your first words. Breathing deeply is very important. Some refer to it as getting the poison out. However, it must be done discreetly. If done in a very noticeable fashion, people may think you are hyperventilating.

Breathe in through the nostrils and out through the mouth. Continue to do this for as long as it takes to feel comfortable. To really take your mind of your upcoming presentation, count the number of breaths you take. This helps to relax you and ensures a stronger, more forceful voice as you speak your first words.

Another relaxation technique is to think of your favorite vacation spot just prior to your presentation. Think of a place and time where you were extremely calm and relaxed.

I personally enjoy grilling out in my backyard. On a nice, sunny day, there's nothing I enjoy more than grilling. That's a form of relaxation for me. Therefore, when I am a bit tense just prior to my presentation, I focus on grilling out in my backyard, while breathing deeply. In my own mind, I'm in the backyard. I feel the wind blowing. I smell the aroma of the food being grilled. That is very relaxing for me.

It's imperative to remain as relaxed as possible prior to your presentation. It is necessary to do a great opening. Besides, if you have completed all of the other steps I have outlined earlier, there's nothing more to do. You are fully prepared. There's no need to sit and worry about your presentation. You are going to do just fine.

Chapter 4

Speech Preparation: Seven Easy Steps

Many people dread the speech preparation part of the speaking business—so much so, they decide not to prepare—"winging it" as it's referred to, or speaking off the top of your head. For most people, this is a costly mistake.

There are only a gifted few that can "wing it" and really impress an audience. And even then, it's not what it appears to be. Most have used parts, if not all of the speech some place before.

Actually preparing for your presentation can be quite enjoyable, if you know how to prepare. I have simplified the process in seven easy steps.

Speech Preparation: Seven Easy Steps

Select The Topic
Develop The Body
Tailor The Speech
Create The Close
Prepare The Opening
Add Spice
Practice Again, Again And Again

Figure 4.1 Speech Preparation: Seven Easy Steps

Step #1—Pick A Topic

The topic that you select is the first critical step in the speech preparation process. In selecting the topic ask yourself these questions: What's my objective? What's the purpose of the speech? What do I want to accomplish? Am I going to inform or do I need to persuade and motivate, or a combination of these?

Entertainment was intentionally left out on purpose, primarily because every speech should have some entertaining qualities. If your sole purpose is to entertain (i.e., a stand-up comedian), there is still value in reading this book; however, this information is not geared toward comedy acts.

There are always answers to these questions and occasionally these decisions may have been made for you in advance. For example, you are the keynote speaker for a special event where the theme has been selected.

The organizers may ask you to speak on a certain topic or they may simply say this is the event and here is the theme for the event. As a speaker, you should always have the latitude to determine how you will approach a certain topic. That should not be dictated to you; however, you will receive suggestions.

In cases where the theme has been selected for you, it's important to mention it throughout your presentation. This at least gives the audience the impression that the speech was specifically designed for this occasion, even if it wasn't.

Many great speakers will take a canned speech and insert themes strategically throughout the speech. I will speak more about this in "customizing your speech."

It's also important to ask yourself, "What do I want

my listeners to do differently?" If your intent is to have your listeners to continue to do what they have always done, then obviously you just need to motivate them to stay on the same path. However, if your purpose is to convince them to do something differently, then that requires a whole different arsenal. The topic that you present should be based on what your audience wants or needs to hear. If you have no idea as to their wants or needs, then consult the person responsible for booking you for the event.

Otherwise, you may contact a sample of the people who will be in attendance and inquire about their desires and expectations. Additionally, this allows you to customize your presentation.

If the topic has already been selected for you, fully examine why it was chosen and why you were selected to present it.

Additionally, in selecting a topic it is important to select something that you feel passionate about. Most anyone can do research and give a presentation about most any subject, but it's passion that will help to create enthusiasm and intensity.

For example, anyone can give a presentation on the use of computers. But, do you have a passion for talking computers? My point is, it's not good enough to simply research a topic and think that it can be delivered with passion. It's not that simple.

Determine what's catchy, what's faddish? Depending on the occasion, you may want to go with glitz or you may opt to avoid it. You do attract the interest of more people if you go with something really catchy.

Additionally, if the topic of your presentation will be used in advertising, you want something that will capture the attention of the masses. And, the masses is what you want, particularly if this is a paid function, for your sponsor.

You always want your sponsor or host to be successful in having you to speak at their event. If they are successful, you're successful.

Also, if you are speaking at an event where there are concurrent sessions and you are competing with other speakers, you truly want a topic that will draw people. I frequently train at these types of events and prefer having an overcrowded room versus a sparsely populated one.

Generally, this has more to do with a catchy title rather than anything else. With all else being equal and if you are an unknown, a catchy title can work wonders for you.

Personally speaking, I don't like being the speaker that has to have an audience rounded up with extras from the hallways in order to have enough participants to go forward with a session.

Step #2—Develop The Body

The best way to develop the body of your presentation is to focus on your topic. Spend five minutes brainstorming or mind-mapping for main points. Write down everything associated with this subject mater. Write it down as soon as you think of it.

Don't take the time to try to determine if it makes sense. That will only stifle your thinking. Write them down as they occur. Don't even take the time to correct misspelled words. With effective brainstorming and mind-mapping, you will have some ideas that will not be usable, but that's okay.

After five minutes, go through and edit your thoughts. In review, you will find that some of your thoughts will be out in left field. That's okay. It simply means that you have done an effective job in brainstorming.

Now, you should go through and decide upon three main points. You don't need seven or eight main points. You only need three. Can you imagine getting up before an audience saying, "I have eight main points I would like to share with you today?"

On the other hand, if you were to say, "I have three main points to share with you on today," that is much more palatable to an audience. Besides, your audience is much more likely to remember three points than eight.

After you have selected your three main points, you must then organize them. All that's left is to provide supporting information for each of your main points: Main point number one and supporting information. Main point number two and supporting information. Main point number three and supporting information. Keep in mind that main points should always include stories, examples and personal experiences.

Once this is done, you have the meat of your speech. If you discover, however, that you need additional material to lengthen your speech, add stories and examples rather than additional main points.

It's helpful to always be in a speech collecting mode. As you are reading the morning paper, attending banquets, listening to your radio or watching television, jot down information that can be used in your next speech. It's to your advantage to have more ideas and information than needed when preparing your speech.

Step #3—Tailor The Speech

Homework or research is a prerequisite for a good presentation. Your audience wants to know that you understand their special needs and desires. Cavett

Robert, the founder of the National Speakers Association, says, "They don't care how much you know, until they know how much you care." This is a very true statement.

Even if 95 percent of your speech is "canned," it's that extra 5 percent of tailoring that makes all the difference in the world.

Dr. Norman Vincent Peale, the author of *The Power of Positive Thinking*, says, "I give the same mashed potatoes for each speech, I just change the gravy."

Of course, the key to tailoring your speech is knowing your audience and the organization. It is imperative that your audience feels as if the speech was specifically designed for them. Visiting an organization's website can be tremendously helpful in gathering information.

In order to do this, however, you must do some research. This is done by learning as much as possible about the audience in advance. You must know who they are, their interests, their needs and expectations.

As a last resort, this may be done in greeting people or during the program prior to your presentation. Always keep a pen handy to write down names and stories that will be shared with you. Take advantage of these opportunities. They almost always occur. Just be prepared.

This is another reason why it's important to interact with your audience prior to your speech. Valuable information that you pick up through conversation can be quite useful.

As previously mentioned, if you really want to make your audience feel good about you during your speech, use names of individuals that you have met at the function. Remember, there is no sweeter sound than the sound of a person's name.

Also, you may have opportunities to tie in some of your information with the previous speaker. This is an opportunity to create the perception that your presentation was specifically designed to fit right in and complement the others.

As a speaker for a particular event, you may have some general knowledge as to who the people are that may be attending. However, you should still do your research. To do this, the first thing to do is inquire about the audience through the person that asked you to speak. Questions that need answering are:

1) What are their expectations?
2) What is their depth of knowledge
   in the specific subject area?
3) What are their interests?
4) Who will speaking before you?
5) Who will be speaking after you?
6) Is there a theme?
7) How long are you expected to speak?
8) How often do you have these events?

Remember, the audience shouldn't have to pick the portions of your speech that are useful to them. It is your responsibility as a speaker to provide useful information throughout your speech.

Take advantage of any opportunity to share with them any common experiences. Additionally, if you have similar backgrounds or if you can relate through family experiences, let your audience know it. The ultimate goal is to have them to feel that you are one of them. That's the ultimate acceptance or approval.

Use terminology and acronyms that are familiar to the audience. Personalize it. This is an opportunity to use the names and information that the audience has shared with you during the meet and greet process. It may be information that you have picked up from research or the program questionnaire.

Whenever you are asked to speak at an event, you should immediately complete a program questionnaire. It will aid you in determining whether you should accept the invitation or not and it also has pertinent information that every speaker should have prior to speaking to any audience.

An example of one is shown below. The questionnaire should be modified, depending on your specific needs.

Program Questionnaire
General Information

Date of contact _________________________ Time _________________

Contact person's name ______________ Title _________________

Organization's name_______________________________________

Organization's address ______________________________________

Website ____

Phone ____________ Fax ____________ E-mail _______________

Name of the event ____

Event's theme ____

Expectations by having me as speaker_____________________________

____

Speaker before me ____

Speaker after me ____

Previous speakers ____

Misc.____

____

____

Audience Analysis

Number attending? _____ Education _____ Average Age ____

Male/Female Ratio _____ Hobbies/Interest _______________

Length of time employed ________________________________

Titles_______________ _______________ _______________

Three things I should know about your organization _________

____

____

Challenges facing your organization _____________________

____

Jargon & acronyms I should know _______________________

____

____

Logistical Information

Event's location _____________________________________

Directions ____

____

Date of speech ______ Time ________ Length of speech ______

Equipment provided ___________________________________

Misc.____

____

Miscellaneous

____

____

____

____

____

____

Figure 4.2 Program Questionnaire

Step #4—Create Your Close

The close is the most important part of your speech. The close is your destination. It's truly unfortunate that a lot of people don't realize this. It is the part of your speech that is used to get the results you want.

Good speeches can lose their effectiveness because of a poor closing. Speeches that end with, "Well, that's all I have to say" or "My time is about up," don't leave a positive impression with the audience. Those are sure signs of novice speakers.

Have you ever been listening to a speaker, then he suddenly ends his speech with, "Thank you very much?" You had no idea the speech was ending. Or just the opposite, the speaker says, "As I close," then a few minutes later, he says, "As I close" again.

It's irritating when speakers promise to close and don't. This is done for a number of reasons. They know that alertness increases when a person hears "As I close" or "As I take my seat."

Some speakers will say it for that very reason. They may look out into the audience and realize the audience appears to be bored or even worse people have fallen asleep.

By the way, to have people to fall asleep during your presentation is not the worst thing that can happen to you. There are plenty of things that are worse.

Other speakers may do this with genuine intentions of closing their presentation. However, a new idea occurs to them and they feel compelled to share it. They are simply excited and are attempting to share with you as much information as they possibly can.

The closing should be memorized. I repeat—the closing should be memorized. This is no time to hem-haw around. Here is where you deliver the knockout punch. With the ending memorized, you will appear polished and your closing will have more impact.

There are various types of closings that can be very effective. Let's discuss a few of them:

1) Future prediction—This method is most effective when you explain to the audience where they are today in your opening, support it with facts in your body, then you tell them what things will be like in the future.

I have seen speakers use this closing very effectively, particularly politicians. The general message is vote for me and I'll make a difference. You'll see. The success of this method largely depends on how well you have judged your audience's perception of current conditions.

2) Emotional Close—Don't be bashful about putting emotions into your close. If you truly want to move your audience to action, show emotions. In fact, it's extremely difficult to convince an audience to see your point of view without it.

3) Quotation or Scripture Close—Using quotations during your close can add authority, amuse your listeners, and add punch. Quotation closes should be a quote of someone with whom your audience can identify.

However, that isn't always necessary. If the quote is powerful enough and seems as if it was specifically written for the occasion, use it. Even if your audience has never heard of the person that you are quoting.

In using quotes, make sure you get them right. Remember, if this is someone that your audience can identify with, chances are they have heard the quote before. So, they will know if you misquote.

The same is even more critical in using scriptures from the Bible. I was attending an event sometime ago and the speaker said, "I can do all things through God, who strengthens me."

Several members of the audience made nasty facial expressions and mumbled following that statement. They obviously knew the Bible well. I don't know if the speaker realized what he had done wrong, but I'm sure he noticed the feedback. People can be unforgiving in misquoting the Bible.

4) Tell a story—A powerful story can make a memorable close, particularly a personal story or a story of someone with whom the audience can identify. It's always good to personalize stories to get the most from them.

Think of events that have happened in your life and share them with your audience. Some speakers are skilled at taking incidents that have happened to others and making them their stories. I have seen this practice used very effectively, although I disagree with this concept. We all have our own stories. We just need to refine them. Nevertheless, telling a story can be the most effective of all closings. Stories are powerful! This is actually my favorite.

5) Rhetorical question—This method can be powerful; however, I have seen people give a great presentation and use this closing very ineffectively.

For example, after outlining the problem and sharing the factual information, the speaker will say, "And, now what are you going to do?"

And, he will take his seat. Well, what do you want

them to do? This closing can be effective, but requires the right presentation and skills to be employed.

6) Summarize your points—Repeat in a very abbreviated form the points you discussed in the body of your presentation. Repetition helps your audience to remember what was said. In fact, it has been said to tell the audience what you are going to tell them, tell them, and then tell them what you told them.

Here are some things to keep in mind at closing:

1) Never overstay your welcome—meaning close your presentation on time. If you have been given the amount of time to speak and you usually will be, adhere to that time period, even if you are "bringing the house down."

Even if you know they are loving you, close on time. If there is a need for you to continue beyond the allotted time, the sponsor or organizer will sense this from the audience and may ask if they want you to continue, but never make this decision on your own.

As an invited speaker, you don't have the authority to make such a decision. On the other hand, if you have been given "free reign," you must be able to determine by the feedback from your audience when it's time to go.

A good rule of thumb is to always leave your audience wanting more.

It's quite appalling to attend functions and see a speaker yell over to the Master of Ceremony "I know my time is up, but I just have to say this." No, you don't. You can and should take your seat.

It's important to always close on time. There are many reasons to do so, but I will mention just two of them: (A) Someone is responsible for keeping the event on time. That person certainly would appreciate your cooperation. (B) It's very likely that someone follows you as a speaker. That person deserves to give his presentation without being pressed for time or having to shorten it due to your inability to end at the allotted time. Additionally, that person is probably sitting back calmly, but wishing that you would complete your presentation and take your seat.

Many experienced speakers actually try to end their presentations a few minutes before the allotted time. Audiences tend to like that.

If you end too early, however, it can create a logistics problem for the coordinator. Bear this in mind when making this decision.

2) Never go on and on at closing. In other words, don't ramble. By the way, people do recognize this. Audiences appreciate speakers that finish early as compared to speakers that go beyond the allotted time.

Speakers typically start to ramble when one of the following occurs: (a) The speaker has become very comfortable; (b) The speaker has gotten in hot water and is trying to cleverly smooth things over prior to ending the speech.

Speakers that tend to ramble, many times, will end up putting their foot in their mouth. Additionally, rambling is a sure way of getting off track and losing your audience.

3) Never introduce new information at closing.

The time to introduce new information is not at closing. That's a new speech altogether.

Even if your purpose is to simply whet the appetite, it can be counterproductive to your current presentation. There may be times when you have accidentally left out information during your presentation; you must determine if it is necessary to add it at the end or to leave it out altogether.

This becomes extremely important, particularly if you have announced your closing.

Additionally, it could create a tremendous amount of confusion for your audience in determining how the new information should fit in.

If you determine that the information is critical and must be presented, then it's imperative that the audience understands where the information fits.

A prime example of this would be a situation in which you are presenting information in steps. For example, step one, step two, step three, etc. However, during your close you realize that step two was inadvertently left out and the outcome will be greatly affected without this step.

In this case, add it in and let your audience know where it fits. On the other hand, if you have left out information that's not critical and it doesn't undermine the integrity of your speech, leave it out.

4) Never close with a question and answer period.

Whenever I say this in my seminars I always get raised eyebrows. Many people will say, "I always close my meetings or presentations with a question and answer session."

Please don't misunderstand me. I'm not saying you shouldn't have a question and answer session. I'm simply saying, do not allow that to be your close.

If you are going to have a question and answer session and many presentations lend themselves to that, do that just prior to your closing.

The reason being: you want people leaving your

presentation thinking about the last thing that you said, not the last question that was asked. People tend to remember what they hear last. You always want people to leave your presentation thinking about what you said last, not what someone else said.

After all, the purpose of your presentation was to inform or persuade and motivate.

It's always important to remain available for your audience after your presentation. Frequently people leave events right after their presentations, particularly politicians. Not only do they not wait to interact with their audience members, many times they don't even wait until the end of the program to leave.

Remember, your audience always wants to speak with you. Never deny them this opportunity. There will be people who would like to shake your hand and to simply thank you for speaking to them.

There may be occasions where there will be people that will know relatives of yours, or may have attended the same school, etc. They always want to share this information with you.

I mentioned this recently in one of my seminars and there was a state senator present. He said, "But, you don't know how many of these events we have to speak at." I said, "You're right, I don't, but if it were election time you would stay and shake hands wouldn't you?" "Oh, yeah," he replied.

Step #5—Prepare The Opening

The opening is the second most important part of your presentation. You should start with a bang. Always remember that you have just one opportunity to make a good first impression. Take advantage of it.

Your audiences' interest and attention are at their

highest at the beginning of your presentation. They will allow you two to three minutes to really impress them. They make major decisions within this time frame.

Bear in mind, your audience will be thinking about a number of things. Your goal is to get them to focus on you and your message. Some techniques for doing this are: make a startling statement; ask a rhetorical question, tell a joke, a story or anecdote; or begin with a quotation.

My personal favorite, and that of many speakers, is to tell a joke. It loosens up the audience and creates a certain degree of comfort for the speaker. Of course, jokes may or may not be appropriate depending on the situation. You'll have to be the judge of that.

I remember attending a conference about ten years ago. Many people regretted going to this particular conference because it was notorious for boredom. Being fully aware of this reputation, the opening speaker decided to do something about it.

About five minutes into his presentation he took off his coat. At the ten-minute mark, he took off his necktie. Fifteen minutes into his presentation, he took of his shirt. Do you think anyone was thinking this was a boring conference? Absolutely not.

In fact, people were wondering how far he was going to go. I'm sure, there were some saying, "Go ahead, go ahead, go ahead." Obviously, his actions were quite unusual. Nevertheless, he was able to hook the audience from the outset.

By the way, the speaker had a tee shirt on with the conference's theme on the back. I thought, "Wow, what an idea?" What a way to start out a conference that had been branded as boring. I still remember that opening as if it were yesterday. The speaker obviously set the pace for the entire conference. Even though it took more than one speaker and one conference to erase years of earning that title, this one speaker did a lot in charting a new course, however.

As a speaker you have to hook your audience right away. Your audience will allow you two to three minutes to "show and tell." Unfortunately, those first few minutes are when speakers experience the most nervousness. That's why it's imperative to have your opening memorized.

The beginning of your speech should indicate what you will be talking about and why your audience should be interested. When audience members understand the topic and how they will benefit from listening to your speech, they will immediately pay close attention.

Remember, you must sell benefits. We all have heard of the most popular radio station in the world (WIIFM)—Meaning, "What's In It For Me." As a speaker, you must know and understand that people will take an interest in your speech for their own benefit and interest.

Things to avoid in your opening:

1) Starting late—there will always be people that will arrive late. By the same token, there are always people that will be there on time and early. It's important to show your audience that you respect their time by starting on time.

It's important to start on time, even if the house isn't packed. Whenever you don't start on time, you risk the chance of causing the audience members that were on time to feel that you really don't value their time or they are not as important as those who were not on time.

Second, it sets a precedent for future events. For example, if you start on time, in the future people will know that they should be there on time. Otherwise, they're going to miss a portion of the program.

However, if you delay the event, it gives the impression that there is no need to attend on time.

Of course, this depends on whether you actually have this kind of control. Many times as a speaker, you don't. When I am the guest speaker at events and the host asks if I would like to go ahead and start even though more people are expected, I always say "yes." Pick a starting time and stick with it.

2) Never start with an apology.

Don't apologize for anything. If something terrible happens, your audience will see it and know you are sorry. They know that if it was something you could have controlled, you would have.

They understand that. If it's a small error, they probably won't notice it anyway, unless you bring it to their attention by apologizing. Therefore, don't. Apologies are negatives. Never begin a presentation with a negative.

It burns me up to have a speaker to get up before a group and make an apology for not being ready. I hear people say, "I learned on yesterday that I had to do this presentation," obviously meaning they are not prepared.

Another popular one is to say, "I'm nervous, so please bear with me." Never, never do this. It is interpreted as a forewarning for a terrible presentation or as a request to lower your expectations. It really doesn't work.

Avoid telling the audience in your opening statement about all of the terrible things that have happened to you preventing you from being adequately prepared.

For example, I had planned to prepare for this engagement last night, but my son wrecked the car and my daughter missed the bus this morning.

People have their own problems and don't much care to hear about others. If you don't believe that, just ask them. People's time is still being consumed; therefore, their expectations remain unchanged.

3) Never start with unrelated jokes or humor.

People frequently comment in my seminars that they always start their presentations with a joke. I think this is a good idea, by the way. It's important, however, that the joke is related in some way to your speech.

Jokes or some form of humor is an excellent way to start your presentation. It relaxes you as a speaker and it also relaxes your audience.

Incidentally, there is never a good reason to use unrelated jokes or humor, primarily because most humor can be tastefully tied into almost any presentation. Generally, this can be done with a sentence or two and a little bit of forethought.

4) Don't forget to set the hook.

Think of it as fishing. You have got to set the hook in your opening. When you open with a bang that is setting the hook, and remember the audience is always "a keeper."

In your opening, you have to capture your audience; otherwise, you are going to be fighting a losing battle during the remainder of your presentation.

5) Never open by testing the equipment.

It is critical that you make sure your equipment is

working properly prior to your presentation. The best way to ensure this is to test it.

Even though this will not be a 100% guarantee, it is a good practice. I can't overemphasize the importance of testing the equipment prior to the actual presentation.

I have seen people testing equipment at the beginning of their presentation—testing 1,2,3; testing 1,2,3; testing 1,2,3. This is quite unprofessional. The time to do this is not at the opening of your presentation, but well before.

No matter how well you have prepared, if your microphone fails, if the bulb on the overhead projector blows, additional stress is created. If something breaks, don't stop and repair it. Acknowledge the problem and move on.

People do understand that accidents happen; what they don't understand is having to wait while you fix it. Give some thought and be prepared for any situation that may result from equipment failure. It's imperative that you have a backup of some type.

Step #6—Spice It Up

Spice is necessary to keep your audience alert. Spice can be in many forms. For example, spice can be jokes, games, music, props, stories, visual aids, activities, skits, give-away items, and mind teasers.

Vocal variety can also be a form of spice. The list is endless. Some speakers use magic and audience participation as forms of spice. I have even seen speakers sing. I would never attempt to sing for fear of my audience walking out.

The adult attention span is five to seven minutes.

Understanding how your audience's attention span works is the key to rave reviews.

The attention level is highest at the beginning and end of a presentation. That's why it's critical to make a good first impression and a dynamic closing. If you start off on the wrong foot or if you lose your audience in the beginning of your speech, recovery is almost an impossibility.

It's important to understand that even the best speakers must use spice. Many times, that's why speakers are labeled as "good" or "dynamic," it's because of the use of spice.

If you should happen to start losing your audience, it's important to understand the necessity of spice. Zig Ziglar says he uses spice every six to eight minutes to bring people back into his presentation. I spoke earlier about some speakers' continuous use of "As I close" as a form of spice. That is their way of bringing people back into their presentation.

The speakers that do this understand that the attention level of an audience always increases when they think the presentation is about to come to a close. Therefore, they use that as a way of increasing the attention level of the audience as it starts to sag.

However, I advise against that. Never lead your audience to believe you are closing when you are not. Rather than mislead, use spice.

Audience members' minds will start to drift with even the best speakers. If it happens to you, it doesn't mean you are not a good speaker or they are not interested in what you have to say.

It's only normal that during the body of your speech, the interest level goes down. The reason is the average presenter speaks about 130 to 180 words per minute. If fewer or more words are spoken then he is speaking at a pace that is too slow or too fast.

However, the average person can comprehend from 600 to 800 words per minute. So, your audience is thinking about four times faster than you can give them the information to think about. That allows time for the mind to wonder.

Therefore, after you have prepared your speech, go back and add some form of spice throughout. Spice will be used to bring them back into your presentation.

Special Note: Once you are finished writing your speech, set it aside for a while. It's best to set it aside for a day, but if that's not possible, make it at least two hours. That way, you are allowed to take a break and focus on something else. When you return, you will always have different and better ideas. It works every time.

Step #7—Practice Again, Again And Again

If the professionals have to practice, what about you? A question I frequently get is, how much practice is necessary? The answer is very clear; practice as many times as it takes to become comfortable with your presentation.

Practice enough so that if someone were to ask you to give your presentation on the spot, you could give it without hesitation (or even asking why). That may mean five times or it could mean 20. Your comfort level increases with each practice. With that in mind, how many times will you practice, five or 20?

If you have decided to speak at an event, you owe it to yourself as well as your audience to give it all you have to give. I have advised countless people that had previously put together a quick presentation and delivered it with little to no practice.

At best, they received a lukewarm reception. Then they become completely turned off by public speaking. They don't understand that the skilled and poised speakers are the ones that have done their homework and practice.

Plain and simple—practice is the single most important step in becoming a good public speaker.

Always, and I repeat always, allow yourself enough time to adequately practice. The most relaxed, confident speakers are not just naturally poised; it's a result of effective practice.

When I say effective practice, I don't just mean reading over your notes, studying material and memorizing parts of your presentation. All of this helps, but these steps alone don't constitute effective practice.

There Are Four Simple Steps To Practicing Your Speech

Refine Your Speech
Mental Rehearsal
Practice Alone
Practice For Feedback

Figure 4.2 Four simple steps to practicing your speech

1) Refine Your Speech

Make sure your speech is as complete as possible. This doesn't mean there will not be changes as you practice your speech. In fact, there should always be changes during your practice, primarily because as you practice you'll discover that there are certain words that do not flow as well as you would like.

This may very well happen because of the differences in the way that you write and speak. However, if you have written it in a conversational style, your changes will be minimal. If you find certain words causing problems for you as you practice, replace them immediately because they will also cause problems during the delivery of the actual presentation.

You'll also discover that some words don't have the desired effect. Now is the time to replace them. Go through your presentation carefully to make sure it is as complete as possible.

I personally like to write my entire speech word-for-word before starting to practice. This is what works best for me.

I do know some speakers that simply develop an outline and ad-lib their speech. I very rarely do this. I only do this when I am extremely familiar with the material, which means I have presented it many times before. That way, it's not necessary to write the speech word-for-word.

However, I don't recall the last time I started a speech from scratch. Over the years, I have used some of the same information over and over. I simply cut and paste with my computer.

If you ever have the opportunity to follow a professional speaker from city to city, you will find that he is repeating the same speech with only minor modifications. There is absolutely nothing wrong with doing this.

There is no rule or law in public speaking that says you must deliver a new speech to each audience. In fact, I highly recommend that you not do this. If you have discovered, based on previous presentations, that certain parts of your speech are tremendously appreciated by your audience, use them time and time again.

If it always gets a roaring laughter or a thunderous applause, use it. That's what the professionals do. I only caution you to be mindful of the audience and not give them the same speech repeatedly.

I went to see Zig Ziglar at a seminar in Washington, D.C. in 1993. I went to see him again in Jackson, Mississippi in 1997. Some of the same information he presented in 1993, he presented in 1997. Since he has been in the public speaking arena for more than 30 years, I suspect some of the material he uses has been a part of his presentation for nearly that length of time.

I see nothing wrong with it. The bottom line is if it's appreciated and continues to accomplish the objective, use it.

I have discovered that each time I use the same material, I present it a little better. You will realize this, too. Therefore, the goal is to use effective material and continue to use it with minor changes to create the illusion that the material was specifically designed for the current event.

Even though you may present the same material over and over again, it must still be presented with freshness. Although you should make changes as you practice, avoid last minute changes wherever possible. This almost always causes disaster.

2) Mental Rehearsal

It's important that you can mentally see yourself giving this speech from beginning to end. In your own mind, you must walk through your speech step-by-step. Make sure everything is in place.

Determine at what point you are going to use visual aids.

Decide if you have inserted spice frequently enough. Figure out what points need emphasizing. Make sure you are ready logistically.

Mental rehearsal is a practice that is done by coaches all the time. They will have players to mentally walk through various plays before they do anything physically. They want them to see it happening in their mind's eye first.

Part of the mental rehearsal process is to also visualize your audience and the room in which you will be speaking. After this step is completed, you are ready physically.

Sports teams usually win most of their home games because of familiarity. It's referred to as the home court or home field advantage. As a speaker, you must learn to feel comfortable in a strange environment.

There's no better place for rehearsing than in the actual room where you will be delivering the presentation. However, most of the time that's not practical. In that case, practice in a similar room. If you don't have access to a similar room, use the power of your imagination.

In practicing, see yourself in the very room of your presentation. Nevertheless, you should always get into the actual room and get acclimated before the presentation.

3) Practice Alone

Practice with index cards or sheets of paper.

Depending on your preference you can use 3x5 or 5x8 index cards or 8½x11 sheets of paper.

There are advantages and disadvantages in index cards and sheets of paper.

Obviously, one advantage with sheets of paper is the ability to put more information on them. Additionally, many speakers like to carry slick, notepad-type folders that can be easily situated on the podium or lectern. However, the index cards are much more portable.

In preparing your notes, write down key words and phrases. Don't write entire sentences. Your notes should be used to prod your memory. If one word will do the job, then use just one word. However, if more words are needed, then use more. Be sure the print is clear and large enough for you to understand it at a glance.

Organize your notes in the order of your presentation. Be sure to number the cards and pages, if there are more than two. By the way, if you do have more than two pages of 8½x11 sheets, you have too many.

If you have more than three to four index cards, taking in consideration the size of your print, you probably have too many index cards. However, if you feel you must have them for a safety net, go ahead and use them. It will only be a matter of time before you feel comfortable with fewer.

The reason for numbering the notes or index cards is purely a precautionary measure just in case you drop them.

If you do drop your notes or index cards, it is never a convenient time. Hopefully, it will not be as you are preparing to deliver your presentation. I have seen that happen. Once it happens, it will seem to take a lifetime to pick them up and put them back in order.

Writing down keywords and phrases on the index cards or papers will be a way to remind you of your speech, as opposed to using all of your notes during a presentation.

Once you've worked with your notes a few times, you'll begin to memorize the information. In a best case scenario, you'll carry a mental image of these cards in your presentation.

But, even if you don't, you can put them in your purse or pocket and carry them with you to your presentation. The idea, however, is to practice long enough and hard enough that you don't need the index cards.

By the way, never practice with index cards and attempt to deliver your presentation with 8½x11 sheets of paper or vice versa. Practice with exactly what you plan to use during the delivery of your speech.

If you were to look at the notes of some experienced speakers, you would be amazed to find how few notes they use. For them, having notes is like having auto insurance; you rarely need it, but it's comforting to know that it's there for you.

Additionally, practice should include the equipment that you will be using during your speech. I have seen speakers that come before their audience and can't figure out how to turn the overhead projector on. That's very embarrassing.

Equipment can cause mechanical and logistical headaches. If you will be using an overhead projector, practice with it. If you will be using a flip-chart, practice with it.

I recall competing in a speaking contest some years ago, and my routine required me to run around the stage a few times in the opening.

Prior to going on stage, I was outfitted with a lavalier microphone with the transmitter strapped on to my belt. As I was running, the unit fell to the floor and broke. The hotel had only one unit. I had to complete my speech without a lavalier microphone.

In fact, for the remainder of my speech, I had to use a microphone with a stand. That really hampered my style.

Even worse, I was the first contestant. None of the other contestants had the luxury of a lavalier microphone either. They weren't very happy with me. I also recall placing third in that competition. I don't believe the judges were very happy either.

There is no other way to put it; it pays to practice with the equipment that you will be using.

Tip: Draw a happy face on each card or sheet of paper. The reason for this is to remind you to smile. It's very easy to forget to smile during your presentation, because you are so concerned about delivering a dynamic speech. However, you must always remember, that the audience mirrors the speaker. If you smile, your audience will smile back at you. If you look terrified, your audience will look terrified, too. Some speakers even indicate on their notes when to use visual aids and when to use voice inflections. This method may be helpful. However, you should be careful to avoid cluttering your notes.

4) Practice For Feedback

Practice in front of someone or a group of people willing to give you feedback. However, you must bear in mind that with some people you can do no wrong.

For example, if you are practicing in front of your spouse, he or she may tell you that you are doing extremely well, when you really are not. They are loving and want to encourage you to do well. But, in actuality, they are undermining your progress.

On the other hand, there are some people with whom you can do no right. That is, their level of expectation for you is so high that you may not ever be able to do well in their view.

Therefore, it's important that if you are going to practice in front of someone or a group, they should be committed to giving you objective feedback. Practicing in front of people also gets you through the mechanics of moving from mental rehearsal to physical rehearsal.

Another option is to practice in front of a mirror. If this is your preference, you will have to provide feedback to yourself obviously. Can you be objective? It certainly allows you the opportunity to see your facial expressions, gestures and platform movement; however, you obviously have to be looking in the mirror the entire time to evaluate your progress. This is actually the preferred method of some people.

You may also use a tape recorder for practice. However, you must bear in mind that you will only be able to evaluate the way that you sound. You have no way of receiving feedback on facial expressions, gestures and platform movement. Any evaluation is better than none.

Video taping is a practice that is quite popular and quite effective. Many people have camcorders in their closets just waiting for the next vacation or graduation. Dust it off and make use of it.

The advantage to video taping yourself is you actually have the opportunity to evaluate how you look and sound. Additionally, you will have the capability to play it back as many times as necessary to do a thorough evaluation.

The beauty of using a camcorder is (if you can truly be objective), you will have the opportunity to evaluate everything that another person could evaluate.

If you prefer not to practice in front of someone, then at the least practice in front of a mirror or use a tape recorder or camcorder. Remember to smile.

It's important to know the physical space in the room. Walk through the room. Know every corner of it. Additionally, sit in your audiences' seat. Know how the room looks and feels from where they are sitting.

Determine if everyone can see well from their seat. Get to see what you would look like from afar. Estimate how much you must project your voice, if there is no PA (public address) system. Estimate how large you must exaggerate your gestures to ensure they will be seen by all.

Added note: Practice at least once in the wardrobe that you will be wearing, particularly if you expect a lot of physical movement. This may seem minor, but it's very important.

As an example, I gain and lose weight fairly easily. I have a couple of wardrobes that I wear once or twice a year. If I were to wear one of the wardrobes on the day of the presentation, I might not notice the snugness for focusing on other things.

It could be disastrous if something rips while making a large gesture. Don't laugh. It could happen.

To illustrate this point, I usually share this story with my seminar participants. Most people remember a few summers ago when Sammy Sosa and Mark McGuire were competing for the record of the most home runs in a season.

Even for people like myself that don't consider themselves baseball fans, they probably remember this, too. In fact, it has been said that because of the competition for the record, the game of baseball has brought back a lot of fans it lost many years ago due to the baseball strike. I suppose that is true. I'm not a true fan, but I certainly was aware of the competition because of all of the publicity.

At any rate, the story goes: There was a little boy that was caught up in the baseball fever as well. This little boy would practice baseball every afternoon in his backyard. He would don his baseball cap, with a ball in one hand and a bat in the other. *(Gesturing to make sure the audience could visualize the little boy's cap, ball and bat.)*

If you would listen closely, you could hear this little boy talking to himself. The little boy would say very proudly, "I'm the greatest baseball player in the world." Then, he would toss the ball in the air. He would swing and miss. *(I would gesture each time as if I was actually tossing a ball in the air and swinging.)*

Remaining cool and calm, the little boy picked up the ball, threw it in the air again and said, "I'm the greatest baseball player ever!" He swung at the ball again and again he missed. He paused for a moment to examine the bat and ball carefully (Obviously, something was wrong). Then once again he threw the ball into the air and said, "I'm the greatest baseball player whoever lived." He swung hard and missed again. "WOW!," said the little boy "What a pitcher!"

I always get a roar from the audience when I tell this one. I'm not sure where I got the story, but I fashioned it a bit to fit my style. Nevertheless, in being this physical, my point is, you could easily rip your suit or jacket unless you have practiced at least once in the wardrobe and have a feel for its elasticity.

When you get on stage and start gesturing as if you are throwing and swinging, chances are very good that you might rip something. That could be quite embarrassing.

Chapter 5

Major Decision— Manuscript, Notes Or Memorized Speech

I am frequently asked by seminar participants if they should use notes. My answer always is: It depends. It depends of the purpose of your presentation and whether you are truly committed to giving a great presentation. In terms of delivery, there are three types of speeches: 1) Prepared texts or manuscripts; 2) Notes with keywords and phrases and 3) Memorized.

I strongly encourage the novice speaker to use as many notes as needed to reduce nervousness. That might very well mean the prepared texts. However, as you progress and make more speeches, you should wean yourself of exhaustive notes.

You must remember, if you are uncomfortable to the point of delivering a speech that is incoherent, then you must do whatever is necessary to alleviate this problem. In other words, forget the rules and what's best.

It doesn't matter that you have excellent eye contact, if you can't remember your name. That may mean having to read a speech word-for-word. I give this advice reluctantly, because I don't want to encourage anyone to read a speech.

You must always push yourself beyond your comfort zone. That's the only way you will begin to grow and fully develop your public speaking skills.

Nonetheless, it's important to understand the importance of being able to thoroughly convey your message. That's the number one priority. If in the beginning of your speech you are unable to use gestures, vocal variety, eye contact, etc., it doesn't mean you are a terrible speaker. It does, however, mean you have a lot of potential for growth.

Manuscript Or Written Speeches

Remember, if you are going to read a text written speech, you should try to sound as if you are talking, *not* reading.

I understand there are busy people that must deliver speeches almost at a moment's notice or individuals that may deliver two to three different speeches in a day's time. It's difficult to find time to practice. That's understandable, but in those cases it's imperative that the speech is read over prior to delivering it.

Other occasions that might warrant a written speech would be when the sole purpose is to *inform*. No entertainment is required or expected.

An example of this is a budget report where numbers and percentages are used frequently and it's imperative that they are right. It is not expected of the speaker to memorize the presentation. However, in these particular cases, it would be beneficial to provide copies to the audience or at least use visual aids. Numbers start to sound alike after a while.

These are examples where the written text or manuscripts are more appropriate. Written scripts or manuscripts are least effective in motivating and inspiring your audience. It's difficult to convince people that you truly believe in an issue when it's read from text.

Using Notes While Speaking

Using notes with keywords and phrases is the preferred choice of many experienced speakers. The obvious advantages to this method are:

1) You have the opportunity to establish more eye contact with your audience, thereby receiving invaluable feedback that's essential for an exceptional presentation.

2) In the event you should go blank in the middle of your speech, you have readily available information to bail you out. For speakers that have experienced going blank in the middle of a speech, they will admit this is an atrocity.

3) It affords you the privilege to get away from the lectern or podium for a while. This is important in having your audience to accept you as one of them.

This method allows you to glance at the keywords and phrases to provoke a thought as you deliver your presentation. It allows you to deliver an excellent speech in a conversational manner filled with conviction. This method of delivery doesn't require you to memorize your speech, but you must thoroughly practice in order to appear polished and poised. This method is applicable whether you are informing, or motivating and inspiring.

Memorized Speeches

If your goal is to motivate and inspire, having a memorized speech will increase your chances *exponentially*. Even though you should always memorize your opening and closing, you'll enjoy greater success if the entire speech is memorized. However, in delivering a memorized speech, you must be careful not to deliver it as if it were a recording. To help you do this, it's beneficial to write the speech in a conversational style, using contractions.

In memorizing your speech, start word-for-word and sentence-by-sentence. Do not move onto additional sentences or paragraphs until you have thoroughly memorized the current material.

To ensure this has been properly done, you should recite this information just as if you were delivering the speech. If you discover that you need to look at your notes and repeat the process (which you will do many times), go back and do so. Repeat this process time and time again, starting at the beginning of your speech each time. Doing this is time-consuming, but the time invested is worth it when you finally deliver the speech. There aren't many joys in life that compare to a standing ovation.

I have been in countless public speaking contests serving as a contestant, judge, organizer, coach and observer, this is something you must remember: Every adult contestant that is serious about winning has a memorized speech. Judges really don't give much consideration at all to contestants that don't bother to do so.

Of course, exceptions are made for youth. But, even then, there is a direct correlation between the youth that have memorized speeches and the ones that win or become finalists. Therefore, for the youth that I coach, the first thing I have them to do is to memorize their speech. "You are much more likely to impress the judges that way," I advise them.

My advice to you as a speaker is to do the same. You are much more likely to impress your audience. Bottom line: It pays to memorize for effectiveness.

Speaking Styles

People that know me and my aspirations know that I idolize Les Brown. He, in my opinion, is the greatest motivational speaker, ever. So, to some degree I try to incorporate his style of speaking into mine. I do not attempt to become Les Brown because I can't. Besides, if I were to try, I'm sure I would appear superficial and very uncomfortable. The audience has the ability to sense superficial speakers.

Being mindful of other speakers' styles can be beneficial to fully developing your own. It's good to see how others work the audience and try to use some of their techniques to get the same results. In fact, that is part of the learning process—see what others do and make it work for you. That's growing. That's evolving. That's developing.

Les Brown

I was listening to one of Les' tapes recently. He talked about an incident where he was one of several speakers at an event. The theme of the event was consistent with one of his existing programs. Once he realized it, he said, "This will be easy. I already have a tape on this. The only thing I need to do is to insert a few names. Yeah, I already have a speech for this program."

At the event, there was a young lady that was scheduled to speak before him. Prior to going to the podium, she said, "Mr. Brown, I admire your work. I truly admire you. I think you are the greatest." He was flattered by her comments and said, "Thank you. Thank you, very much."

When she started to speak, he immediately realized that she was using one of his speeches, the same one he had planned to use for this occasion. He said to himself, "Waaaaait a minute. That's my speech." He then said to himself, "That's okay. I'll teach her. I'll pick it up where she leaves off and take it out of this universe. I'll teach her."

Well, after listening to her speech, he then said, "She didn't leave me anything. She milked it," he commented. He then said, "Thank goodness, there was a soloist between the speeches." He had to put together another speech.

Well, most people are not like Les Brown. They can't put together another presentation in three to five minutes. In fact, most people will put together a speech and practice it for two to three weeks or two to three months before delivering it.

I strongly encourage my seminar participants to avoid making last minute changes to their speeches. All too frequently it spells disaster. There is difficulty in delivering the speech you have already practiced. Imagine the results in trying to deliver a speech that you haven't practiced.

Only the Les Browns of the world can prepare a speech at a moment's notice—the professionals that are at the top of the speaking arena.

I share this story with my seminar participants, because it is significant to all speakers. Someday, it may happen to them. It happens to most people at some point and time—you have prepared a great speech and the speaker before you delivers your speech or more likely portions of your speech. That's okay. Don't panic. Don't try to make last minute changes. Make plans to deliver your speech just the way you have practiced. It's important that you do this.

Maya Angelou

No one can ever give your speech. Only you can make your speech. Someone else may have a similar message or some of the same points, but only you can deliver your speech.

Even if someone has the identical speech that you have, only you can deliver *your* speech. This point was driven home for me many years ago while attending a beauty pageant in Little Rock, Arkansas.

During the talent contest, there were two young ladies that performed Maya Angelou's poem *Phenomenal Woman*. The first young lady did well, but I think her performance only motivated the other young lady to perform better. The second young lady came out and performed the poem as if she owned it, as if it was hers. She did an outstanding job.

That is what you have to do if you realize that someone is "stealing your thunder." Make it competitive, because your style is uniquely different from anyone else's, even if the words are the same. Your style makes it a different speech.

By the way, if it truly bothers you to repeat some points that a previous speaker has made during the same function, you can simply allude to the wording by saying, "As the previous speaker mentioned..." or better yet, "As Mr. or Ms. said earlier..." It's okay to do that.

It simply emphasizes the point. No, don't try to change your presentation. There is an added bonus to doing this, too; it makes your audience realize that these points obviously are important if two speakers mentioned them.

Remember, we learn from repetition. And, as the participants learn this valuable information, more than likely you will be the one given credit for it, because you were the last one to mention it. People remember what they hear last.

You must always remember, public speaking is a combination of two things: 1) Message and 2) Style.

Message—what you have to present to your audience, your content. There are as many messages as there are people and then more. There isn't much more to be said about that. So, I am going to deal with styles.

Style—how you deliver your speech. Let's use the National Anthem as an example. We frequently hear this song performed at major sports events. The lyrics are the same.

However, imagine how it would be sung by Leontyne Price, an opera singer, Luther Vandross, a rhythm and blues singer, and Willie Nelson, a country singer. Each has a unique or different style of his or her own. Do you think that Willie Nelson will say, "Well, most of the people there will like Luther Vandross' style? Therefore, I will imitate Luther Vandross. Or, for example, if Luther Vandross would say, "Most of the people there will like the style of Leontyne Price. Therefore, I will sing the way Leontyne Price does. No, that doesn't happen.

We all are unique with our own unique style of speaking as these respected singers are with their unique styles of singing. They are famous and are paid very well for their *own* styles.

There are basically two speaking styles: Preacher style and Lecture style.

1) Preacher style—In my seminars, I have participants to put in parenthesis, "Baptist." They seem to get a kick out of that. I am Baptist. I have been a

Baptist my entire life and have grown to love and respect Baptist preachers.

Not to say that other preachers don't exhibit these characteristics, but I relate more to the Baptist preachers because of my background.

My own style of speaking has been greatly influenced, by Baptist preachers. I grew up in the Baptist church listening and wondering how preachers could hold people's attention for an extended period of time. When I say extended, I mean extended (hours at a time).

I remember being in church on Sundays as a small child and listening to our pastor. He could preach for two to three full hours (and sometimes did) in a very entertaining fashion.

These speakers generally appealed to the right side of the brain, lots of stories, anecdotes and personal stories, even humor. The whole purpose was to connect. They did an excellent job at it, lots of touchy, feely stuff. They use lots of gestures, vocal variety and platform movement. The preacher style is a very entertaining form of speaking.

2) Lecture style—For this one, I have the participants to put in parenthesis "college professor." Think back for a few seconds. We all had at least one. The college professor that was extremely intelligent; however, he lacked the true ability to effectively relate to the students. His purpose was to impart information—lots of content. Little to no humor, monotonous voice, very stiff-necked, but full of content—appealing to the left side of the brain.

His thought was, "I should not and will not entertain you. If you don't realize how valuable this information is, it's your loss."

Certainly, all college professors are not this way, just as all Baptist preachers do not exhibit all of the characteristics that were previously mentioned, but each can be justified as an example.

Many speakers that are at the top of their game exhibit characteristics of the Baptist preacher and the college professor.

You don't want to be characterized as a speaker with showmanship only. Speakers of this type, sure enough, will have people leaving their function saying, "Wow, what a great speaker." And, if someone asks, "What did he speak about?" "Oh, oh, oh, I don't remember, but he sure was good."

On the other hand, you do not want to be wooden and regarded as stilted without any entertaining qualities, either. You don't want to look out in your audience and find people are using tooth picks to prop their eye lids open. It's important to have a balance between the two.

Therefore, develop a style that includes both. That's the goal. That should be every speaker's objective.

The Three "Es" Of Public Speaking

Enthusiasm—If you are happy to be speaking to an audience, not only say it, but show it. Here's what Andrew Carnegie, the multimillionaire steel magnate, said about enthusiasm, "Enthusiasm is a great leavening force in the mental world, for it gives power to your purpose. It helps to free your mind of negative influences and bring you peace of mind. Lastly, it inspires personal initiative, both in thought and physical action. It is very difficult for one to do his best when he does not feel and display enthusiasm."

We all have seen speakers that will come to the microphone and say, "I'm so excited to be your speaker for the day," while looking down at their notes with no facial expression to match their remarks.

A typical mental and sometimes verbal response by the audience is, "Yeah right. What's your next lie?" We all are so accustomed to hearing speakers utter these words that they have very little to no meaning anymore. The audience will believe in you only if you are enthusiastic about your presentation.

Empathy—Let your audience know that you know how things look from their perspective. Audiences like speakers who seem familiar. Identify with your audience and prove that you are one of them. Let them know that you understand. This doesn't mean that you should patronize them, only that you should strive to see things from their point of view.

If you are a member of the local PTA and you are speaking to parents, tell them that. If you have teen drivers in your household and you know that the audience does too, tell them about your experience.

Find ways to let your audience know you can relate. Yes, you are one of them. At all cost, however, avoid condescending speeches. I have seen this many times and the unfortunate aspect is I really don't think the speakers realized it. People don't want to be talked down to.

Entertainment or Showmanship—It is not enough to simply give a speech. You must entertain. There is a certain amount of entertainment or showmanship that every speaker must possess. I have seen it and you have too. Musicians have it. Entertainers do, too. However, showmanship in speakers is generally referred to as just a "good speaker."

The speakers that have showmanship are the ones that make you feel what they are saying. They make you see what they have seen. They have the ability to hook you and keep you as they travel through their presentation.

They take you down to the lowest point of the speech, the valley, if you will. They can cause audience members to feel depressed, oppressed, or helpless just as the speaker, as he articulates the experiences. Sometimes they bring audience members to tears.

Equally, though, they have the mastery to take you to the highest peak, the mountaintop, of their speech. Audience members leave their presentation feeling and believing they can conquer the world.

By the way, never end your presentation with your audience in the valley of your presentation.

Be mindful, however, that showmanship doesn't mean being a show-off.

Impromptu Speeches

Thinking and speaking on your feet, speaking extemporaneously, spontaneous speaking. Speaking off the cuff, speaking off-the-top-of-your-head, speaking from your heart. Regardless of how you term it, it generally means speaking without preparation or prior notice.

Do you experience butterflies and noodle knees? Have you ever had to responded extemporaneously, then sat down and said to yourself, "I wish I could do that over?"

Well, it's not unusual to feel that way. Most people do at some point. Ideas always seem to really flow once you are at your seat. Even the best speakers find it difficult to just stand up and have an audience instantly spellbound.

Fred Allen

Here is something that works well, however. If you are in involved in a meeting, an organization, or a function and you know it's just a matter of time before you are called on to speak, have a plan. Carefully plan your beginning and ending and then fill in the middle with what will have the most impact for the audience in the time allotted. Most ad-libs are thought out well in advance. Comedian Fred Allen says, "My best ad-libs are the ones I rehearsed the most."

If it is expected to be a rather short response, plan it and rehearse. I recall discussing this issue during one of my seminars. There was an attendant that was married to a politician. She mentioned occurrences that happen frequently.

She said that when she and her husband, a state senator, would visit churches in the communities, people would always ask him to speak or share a few words with the church members.

She said he always did. He never turned down an opportunity to speak. That was the politician in him. She said that was okay with her.

However, when her husband was done, they would always ask her to speak. She said, "Now, that wasn't okay." She didn't like speaking in public. I explained to her that she did have choices. There are always choices.

If she continued to go to church with her husband, church members were going to continue to ask her to speak. I advised her to write out a one to two-minute speech. Practice it. Memorize it. Impress the church members.

Extemporaneous responses are seldom extemporaneous. Although it would appear to the church members as if it were extemporaneous, it would actually be a presentation that had been well rehearsed. That's perfectly okay.

The bottom line is: There's nothing wrong with practicing what appears to be an extemporaneous response. I have seen many people that really have impressed others with what appeared to be spontaneous responses.

If you must speak off-the-top-of-your-head, here are some suggestions: As you are gathering your thoughts, as a general rule, it perfectly okay to thank the person who has asked you to make the comments. That is—thank you Madame President or Mister President for allowing me to respond to... If more time is needed, you can always restate the question or subject area that you are about to respond to.

The reason for this is: It allows you time to gather your thoughts. Even if it's a subject matter that you know like the back of your hand, it is still best to take a few seconds to formulate your thoughts and ideas before responding. In other words, you are stalling.

Once you are ready to respond, start with an attention grabber. It could be humor, a story or a very strong statement related to the subject matter.

Humor seems to work best on most occasions. State your point and support it with factual information. Summarize your point and sit down. It is important to keep your response brief.

Have you ever seen someone that rambles on and on in those types of situations? The more they talk the more trouble they get in. Avoid doing this. Just because your response was solicited, it doesn't mean you are expected to preside over the rest of the meeting.

Introductions

Rule #1–Write your own. Never provide someone a bio and simply say, "Pick out the portions that you think are most appropriate." You'll be sorry. Even if you provide them a bio and say, "You don't have to say all of that." Guess what? They are going to read your entire bio anyway, because they don't want to leave out what you may consider important.

I recall an occasion when I was speaking at an event; they asked me to provide them a bio and I did. I also provided an introduction. However, I did specifically say to use the introduction to introduce me. I thought it was understood—big mistake. They actually used my bio for the introduction and never used the introduction. I was stumped.

When I said, write it yourself. I don't literally mean handwrite it. Always have it typed. It's embarrassing to have someone introducing you that can't read your handwriting. Don't laugh, I've seen it done. It is not professional at all.

Rule #2–Keep it short. A half-page, double-spaced 15-point font is plenty. Some seem to believe that the best way to impress an audience is to have a long introduction. It is not the quantity of an introduction that impresses an audience; it's the quality of the speech.

There may be occasions when it's necessary to introduce yourself. If you must do this, the only thing you need to convey is your credibility in the subject matter you are going to present.

Be careful because in the minds of your audience members there is a fine line between establishing credibility and being boastful, cocky or even worse, arrogant. Say just enough to establish credibility.

Additionally, accomplishments that you are proud of can be built into your presentation, but I again caution you on being boastful.

Chapter 6

Knowing Your Audience And Making Them Love You

An audience has to have a reason to listen to you. Why should they listen unless you can give them something at least as valuable as their time? This means that from your audiences' viewpoint your presentation has to answer a simple question up front, really fast.

That question is, "What's in it for me?" However, in order to answer this question, you must know your audience. That means you must do your homework.

To find out who your audience is, you should do the following:

1) Find out as much as you can about your audience members. This includes their interest, age, marital status, education, profession, etc. The more you know, the better prepared you can be.

This information is essential in adequate preparation. If you discover that you are addressing a particular group, then you can tailor your presentation to their particular needs and expectations.

Ultimately though, you have to be accepted and considered one of them regardless of the information you find out. There is always commonality between you and every audience. Find it and work with it.

Additionally, in knowing who the audience members are, you can more appropriately use quotations. The whole idea behind quotations is to make a powerful, dramatic statement that will excite, motive and support your presentation.

2) If possible, talk with people who have attended the event before. Get some ideas and suggestions from them. Ask them about the speaker when they attended.

Ask what he spoke about and how well it appeared to have been received by the audience. Additionally, speak with speakers that have spoken at the event before. Ask them about their presentation and how well they thought it was received by the audience, etc.

3) Pre-poll audience members. This one might seem as if you are overdoing it, but it is worth it. I saw this done recently at a conference I attended.

There was a speaker that was on schedule to do a 50-minute workshop. Months before the workshop, he got the names and addresses of some of the attendees from the conference coordinator. He contacted those individuals and solicited input on his presentation. He asked them what would be most effective and useful for them for the 50-minute time period.

After receiving their suggestions, he designed a presentation around them. He received the best rating of any of the presenters.

4) What's their knowledge of this subject area? This is helpful in determining the level of your presentation. If your audience only has a basic knowledge of the subject area, then you should make sure that you are not speaking above their heads.

On the other hand, if they are quite familiar with the subject area, then you should not bore them with elementary material.

5) What experience, bias or baggage might they bring with them to this presentation? This is a precautionary measure. You may be invited to speak on a subject matter that's a mine field—just waiting to be tripped. Be sure to ask the right questions to avoid this.

Even if you think you know the audience, follow these steps to ensure an effective presentation. On the surface, this may appear to be a lot of work. Actually, it's not.

Most of these questions can be answered by the meeting planner or the person inviting you to speak. Furthermore, a little work in advance to ensure an effective presentation is a small price to pay for all of the accolades and standing ovations you'll receive.

Invisible Line

There is an invisible line between every speaker and his audiences. It separates the two of you and creates a you versus them scenario.

It can also be considered as a wall that separates the two of you. Many times, it certainly serves as such. It creates division. It's the speaker's responsibility to break this wall down. It's very simple to do.

Simply take advantage of every opportunity to get as close as possible to your audience physically.

Then, you and the audience become one—we are in this together. I'm one of you. This is difficult to do if you are on a stage, however. You are not expected to step down, although I have seen it done.

Nonetheless, you should come as close as you can to the edge of the stage. As a general rule, this should be done when it's not necessary to refer to notes or at least making your way back to them when necessary.

Eye Contact

There is no surer way to have your audience to distrust you than by failing to look them in the eyes. You'll be able to connect with some audience members immediately. However, with most of them you'll have to earn a place in their hearts. You can do this through effective eye contact.

No matter how large your audience is, each person wants and deserves your personal attention. Therefore, as a speaker you must make a personal connection with each audience member as if you were speaking to him or her directly. Make them feel really important.

Symbol Of Sincerity

I have heard that the eyes are the windows to a person's soul. It has been said that you cannot trust a person with shifty eyes. Thus, people that are not willing to make eye contact can't be trusted. Furthermore, looking someone directly in the eyes is a symbol of sincerity. The same holds true when you are the speaker.

Many people will go to great lengths to avoid looking the audience in the eyes. They try looking at the audience's forehead or nose. Some try looking at the back wall. Still, I have heard of speakers attempting to look just over the top of people's heads—thinking the audience can't tell the difference.

The question I always ask is: Why go through all the trouble? I still cannot understand this. I actually enjoy looking at the audience. What better way to determine how your presentation is being received?

By effectively using eye contact, you have an influence on their attentiveness. Additionally, their eyes and facial expressions reveal their interest in your message. This gives you confidence and allows you to become more comfortable. On the other hand, if you don't look at them, your message will lose its effectiveness.

You must learn to feed off the audience. It can and will serve as a source of strength and encouragement. If you have ever spoken in a Baptist church, you know what I mean by strength and encouragement.

I have had a number of opportunities to speak in various Baptist churches and the "Amen Corner" has got to be the most encouraging group a speaker can ever ask for. Not only do they give encouragement non-verbally, but they talk back to you. They give you all the confidence in the world.

Eye contact can also help you to overcome nervousness. When you look at your audience and see that they are interested in your presentation, your nervousness will start to diminish.

Feedback

The bond that is established between you and your audience through eye contact creates a dialogue, even though you are the only one that's talking. Through this dialogue, you are constantly receiving feedback whether you realize it and whether you want it or not. This feedback tells you whether the audience understands you.

Eye contact answers the questions—are you holding their attention? Are you performing well? Is your message being accepted? Based on the feedback through eye contact, you can make an immediate adjustment in your presentation, if needed. Eye contact is a vital tool for effective presentations. It can and should be used to monitor your performance.

How you use eye contact is critical. You should never use it sparingly or as a peripheral vision. Also, you should practice enough so that you can take your eyes away from your notes for minutes at a time.

If you use notes, it's distracting to your audience when you are constantly looking up at the audience then down at your notes. At best, you will look like a bird drinking water.

However, it's possible to use your eyes effectively while using notes. It does, however, require practice. You can take advantage of an audience's laughter or silence after an important point to glance at your notes.

Better yet, get into the habit of glancing at your notes just before you end your previous statement. This works best when key words are written about certain points, not word-for-word notes.

Friendly Faces

If you know your material and are well-prepared, this method will be able to keep you going without losing your place in your notes, while maintaining effective eye contact with your audience.

It's particularly important in the beginning to establish a bond with your audience. Do this during your opening statement. For your comfort, you should identify people with warm, friendly faces and focus on them. You will find some in every crowd.

These are individuals that usually have the smiling faces and nodding heads.

I worry about speakers who say they always take people with them to speaking events so they will have friendly faces in the audience. If the only friendly faces there are those you brought with you, there are serious problems—you are not connecting with your audience.

At any rate, maintain eye contact with a warm, friendly face for two to three seconds at a time. Then shift your gaze to another friendly face. It's critical not to maintain eye contact too long, particularly if you do not know the person.

The audience member may get the impression that you are staring and begin to feel uncomfortable. In fact, it could become so uncomfortable that the audience member will lower his gaze or worst of all, try to break the contact by shifting his body.

As you begin to bond with your audience, you will then be able to make eye contact with those faces that are not as friendly.

By the way, you will always find some of them in every audience, too. Do not follow any set pattern. Continue to do this throughout the room. In doing this, it's imperative that each member of the audience feels that you are speaking directly to him or her.

Having grown up in the Baptist church, I have a great deal of respect and admiration for Baptist preachers. They are extremely good at effective eye contact. In fact, I recall an incident that happened in my church many years ago.

A friend of mine said the pastor was talking about him during his sermon. I asked why he felt that way. He said, "Because, the preacher was looking at him." My reply was, "He was looking at all of us." Well, my friend then said, "But, he was looking at me when he made the remark." I said, "He was looking at all of us when he made the remark." "Well, he looked at me longer than he looked at everybody else." He replied. Finally, I asked if he was guilty of what the pastor was talking about. He never answered.

Effective use of eye contact is the trait of a good speaker.

It's very easy and only normal to focus on the smiling faces and the nodding heads. Those are the individuals that give you energy. You are to feed off them.

However, you should never have the audience to feel as if you have a preferred group or section, even though you may. Do not neglect any member of your audience. If you do, they will begin to sense that they are being overlooked. They don't like that. No one does and if you want to continue speaking you can ill afford to neglect any of your audience members.

Also bear in mind, that the audience tends to unconsciously mirror the speaker. So, if you are getting frowns and can't understand why, maybe you are frowning. Try smiling and see if they will smile back at you. My bet is—they will.

Body Language

If you are familiar with public speaking, you probably have heard of the Rule of Communication. The rule states that 55% of what's being communicated is communicated through body language, 38% through tonality and 7% rests in the words themselves.

Ever wondered where this rule came from? Well, it originated from Dr. Albert Mehrabian of the University of California in Los Angles (UCLA). He and his colleagues conducted two studies on communication patterns and published the results in professional journals in 1967. They later followed-up with two books in the early 1970's.

Let's further examine this 55%, 38%, 7% rule. Dr. Mehrabian and his colleagues suggest that 55% of what you are conveying to your audience is conveyed through body language such as gestures, posture and facial expressions.

Have you heard of the expression, "What you do speaks so loudly, they can't hear a word you are saying?" This statement says it all. Your body language speaks loudest. In essence, I hear what you are saying, but I see how you feel. Make sure your body language is congruent with the words you are using.

Thirty-eight percent of what's being conveyed is through your tonality. How do you sound when you say what you are saying? I know people that have difficulty getting along with others, because they have yet to understand the power of tonality.

They may very well have the best of intentions, but are notorious for insulting people. When confronted about the situation, their reply is "I don't know why they are mad, all I said was..." They do not realize that it was not what they said, but *how* they said it.

Only 7% of the information conveyed to others is conveyed through the actual words themselves. Only 7%. Nevertheless, it is still critical to use words that people can understand. There are some people that seem to think that if they use big words during their presentation, it will impress people—not so.

People are impressed when they can understand what you are saying. It has been said that there is something marvelous about solving a complex problem with a simple solution. Therefore, keep it simple.

Avoid the use of acronyms, unless you are speaking to an industry or group and you know, for sure, they understand. If you must use them, however, make sure you explain to the audience what they mean the first time you use them.

That way, they will understand if you use them

throughout your presentation. Also, be mindful of jargons and local lingo. It is best to avoid these to ensure a greater understanding by your audience. Don't assume people will understand what you are referring to when using these.

Being mindful of the 55%, 38%, 7% rule is critical in making your audience love you.

Audience Involvement

Be flexible enough to adjust your presentation based on the feedback from your audience. There are signs of boredom that you should be aware of. If your audience seems attentive, wide-eyed with facial expressions and is nodding their heads in agreement, keep doing what you are doing.

On the other hand, if you see a sizeable number of them resting their chins in their hands, looking out of the window, doodling, folded arms, nodding or actually asleep, it is probably an indication that a change is needed.

These are signs that shouldn't be ignored. A change in pace or shift in gears may be what's needed. You may have overwhelmed them with information or there could very well be other extenuating circumstances at play. Sometimes a stand and stretch or a ten to fifteen minute break will do the trick.

These signs are not always indicative of boredom, though. It's possible to read people the wrong way. For example, I had a gentleman in my seminar to remind me of this. He had a very pudgy stomach.

After my seminar was over, he explained to me that he once got in trouble with a college professor by sitting back in his chair with his arms folded, resting on his stomach.

The professor automatically assumed that he was bored with the class because of his disposition. However, that was not the case at all. He explained to the professor that he uses his stomach for resting his folded arms periodically, while being very much interested in the subject matter.

Additionally, I have seen people that appeared to be staring at the ceiling or out of the window, but were very attentive. This was their way of processing the information that was being presented. Therefore, don't be too hasty in analyzing your audience's disposition. Nonetheless, the best practice is to introduce spice long before signs of boredom occur. This simply requires planning on your behalf.

One sure way to keep your audience alert is to get them involved in your presentation. Here are several ways to do this:

1) Volunteer Exercise—Ask for a volunteer from the audience to assist in a demonstration or to write on the flip chart. A good way to do this is simply to ask for a helper. Always ask, rather than pointing to an individual and requesting assistance.

The main reason for this is some people are very uneasy in front of a group of people, even if it doesn't require speaking. Furthermore, you will always get participants by asking. I think it has to do with the fact that as kids, we all wanted to be the teacher's pet. Everybody remembers those times. We love to help.

I frequently refer to it as a teacher's pet, affectionately, in my seminars. You can easily create a Vanna White with your presentation. This process helps to bring you closer to the audience. This only works when you have created an atmosphere of fun, trust and cooperation, though.

I always have a surprise or reward for the teacher's pet. This can generally be done with less than $2.00 to purchase a candy bar, an apple and a banana.

I usually allow the first helper to select whichever one he wants from the three. The second helper selects from the remaining two and finally the third helper gets the final item. This is always a winner with the audience. However, this can be done with most any kind of treat.

Special Note: Always select items that will be of interest to your audience. That's why it's critical to know your audience in advance. But even if you decide not to purchase items as treats, at least lead the audience in a round of applause when the helper is done assisting you. It makes them feel good.

2) Asking questions—Ask a question of the entire audience. This is a very safe and non-threatening approach, if you don't ask any particular individual to answer. It is done by asking a question and requesting the audience to respond verbally or by a show of hands.

This way, even the most timid person doesn't feel threatened by this action. It can be a way of determining your audience's knowledge of the topic you are about to speak on. Additionally, it can also be a method of loosening up your audience.

For instance, asking a question like, "How many of you have heard me speak before or are hearing me for the first time? Raise your hands please." This one always gets a chuckle from the audience. Another alternative is, "How many of you have children or have been a child at least once in your life? Please raise your hand." This one seems to work well, too.

Another way is to pose a question to a specific audience member. This is an excellent way to get audience participation and to keep them alert. Of course, this may or may not be appropriate depending on the type of presentation you are doing.

Never, and I repeat never, pose a question to an individual in your audience without knowing, for sure, that person knows the answer, unless, of course, you are seeking to make an enemy. Never put an audience member on the spot.

Ideally, if you want to call on an audience member in such a fashion, ask the audience member if he or she would mind if you did so. You should always get permission. This can be done during a break or at the beginning of the session. Make sure they know the answer.

If he or she doesn't, tell him or her the answer. Telling them the answer limits the possibility of you and the participant being embarrassed by unexpected remarks.

If you are giving an informative speech and want your audience to ask questions during your presentation, this method is very effective.

The key is to make it known to your audience at the beginning of your presentation whether it's okay or not to stop you during your presentation to ask questions. Obviously, you would only want to do this with a relatively small group.

But, by all means be careful as you answer the questions, particularly in cases where someone inquires about material that will be covered later. Never say, "We'll get to that later," even if you are making plans to discuss it later.

At the very least, let them know you will be covering it later in a tactful way and then ask if it's okay with them. If you know their name or if they have a name tag, use their name in your reply.

It sounds much more polite—as in, "That's a really good question. I'll be covering that in about five minutes. Is that okay with you, Suzanne?"

They will always say "yes." I always say, "Don't let me get through it without answering your specific question." In saying this, it ensures that person will be listening very carefully when you cover the material. Another approach is to briefly answer the question and mention that the specifics will be covered in detail later.

3) Exercises and activities with the audience—

Activities can range from having your audience to repeat a word or phrase (usually led by the speaker) to having them to complete tasks. I use this technique whenever I give motivational presentations to youth, especially.

As an example, I have a presentation called "DreamPower", which is an anti-drug, anti-violence program that focuses on improving self-esteem.

At the beginning of the presentation, I solicit the help of the youth. They are always eager to assist. I simply say "I'm going to speak with you for a short time today, but I can't make it through my speech without your help. Will you help me?" I always receive a resounding "yes."

Then, I will say "Whenever I do this (Raising my arms and hands toward the ceiling with my pointer fingers extended), I need you to say "DreamPower." The youth seem to get a big kick out of it. It's extremely helpful in keeping them focused during a presentation, particularly if the enthusiasm starts to sag a bit.

Additionally, it serves to keep them alert because they never know when it's expected of them to say "DreamPower."

Exercises and activities can be done at anytime during your speech. One popular way is to use them as ice breakers in your introduction. The activities allow a few minutes for people to get to know each other. They can be in the form of group exercises or pairing individuals.

One example of this is to have the audience members to get to know each other and to use the information to introduce each other. Usually, there are specific questions that the audience members are instructed to ask each other.

Amazingly, people tend to be less nervous introducing others than when introducing themselves. An added benefit to this exercise is friendly relationships are frequently formed. This approach is best used in a workshop or seminar-type format. This is when you want the participants to become comfortable with each other in order to solve problems, create suggestions or to compete with other teams.

However, in using this exercise, you must make the rules and guidelines known upfront. Exercises of this type can quickly get out of hand. Additionally, the groups should be monitored for progress and to make certain that all understand the purpose.

Also, you can have your audience to interact with each other in the event that you are introduced as a speaker and you discover, for whatever reason, that you need a few seconds to get organized.

You can have the audience to shake hands with each other or to look at each other and say, "I'm happy you are here today." I have learned this from some of the best speakers. It buys you a little time, and there are many occasions where a few seconds are all you need.

You may also find this technique helpful if you are a bit too nervous to execute your dynamic opening. The reason this works is the attention is diverted elsewhere, which allows you to regain composure or to do whatever has to be done.

4) Note taking—I have the participants to do this a lot in my seminars. It creates the sense of ownership, primarily because everything they write is theirs. They will take all of the notes with them when they leave. Additionally, this information can be referenced a week, months or even years later.

Most people like to take things with them after attending a seminar or event. Therefore, providing a handout for notes is very much appreciated. The most effective way to do this is to have fill-in-the-blanks worksheets.

These handouts help them to focus on the task. Studies have proven that if participants write information they are much more likely to retain it; therefore, they are much more likely to use it. Always remember that if you want note taking, the way to ensure all can participate is to provide the note paper and sometimes even writing utensils.

Humor

Everyone enjoys a laugh. One of the keys to becoming a good public speaker is to learn to use humor. Typically, when I mention humor, I am referring to the ability to tell jokes or stories. However, humor is not limited to jokes and stories. Humor includes gestures, facial expressions, platform movements, etc.

A frequent question I get is: What to do if you are uncomfortable telling jokes? My response is, "Get over it." I had to and everyone has to. Early in my training days, I used to always say that I couldn't tell jokes or use humor. I thought you had to have a certain personality for that. I said that long enough to believe it. Then I discovered you only have to have a personality, which we all have.

I would have someone else to tell jokes during my training sessions. These people became my crutch. I was extremely dependent on them.

So, ultimately I decided that if I was going to be a trainer and motivational speaker, it was imperative that I learn humor as well.

By the way, I used to do experiments in my training sessions. I would do a seminar without the use of humor and I would do the very same seminar with humor. Every single time, the seminar where humor was introduced would have much better ratings than the seminar without.

Humorous Speech Contests

The way that I got over feeling uncomfortable using humor was to compete in Toastmasters International's Humorous Speech Contests. There was one particular time that I remember vividly. I decided to compete at the last moment. After making that decision, I lost some sleep over thinking about the contest.

I spent a lot of time wondering what I could speak about that would be funny to others. I started to watch comedy shows on TV. I quickly realized that I couldn't use that material (primarily due to the graphic nature of the language). However, it was beneficial to see comedians in action. I was able to observe their body language, their timing and how they worked the audience.

Pizza Man

After a few weeks of pondering, I remembered reading someplace that the best humor is humor about yourself. With that in mind, I drafted a speech about my days in college and working at Pizza Hut.

In essence, the speech was about how I became popular with the young ladies in college by using left-over pizza. "Hello, Peggy, what are you doing this evening? By the way, I have a large pepperoni and sausage pizza. Would you like to share it with me?" It worked every time.

The speech was entitled "Pizza Man." Yeah, I know, I could've been more creative with the title. But, I won the humor speech contest at the club level, at the area level, at the division level and placed third at the district level. The district included Mississippi, Arkansas and Tennessee. I was amazed!

By winning those humorous speech contests, it did a lot for my self-esteem. I came to realize that I could do humor. We all can.

When people tell me they can't do humor, my reply is "Yes, you can." The way to get over feeling uncomfortable in using humor is to use it over and over again. Use it when you are uncomfortable. Use it with your spouse and friends. Use it with co-workers. The more you use it, the more comfortable you'll become.

I have discovered, for me, the best way to use humor is in storytelling, rather than jokes with punch lines.

Therefore, the way to start is to tell stories about yourself. Think back into the past. Be sure your stories are in the embarrassing category, not the boastful category. But, remember humor is more than just telling a joke.

Hugging Your Audience

Someone said it best when he or she said think of humor in this way: When you use humor, you are hugging your audience; when your audience laughs, they are hugging you back. I can't think of anyone who doesn't like hugs. Everybody loves humor.

In using humor there are some rules you should keep in mind, however:

1) You must be comfortable—Have you ever seen someone that attempted to tell a joke and it was obvious that he was very uncomfortable with it? It showed all over his face.

Therefore, it's critical to become comfortable with your humorous material before attempting to deliver it to an audience. How do you become comfortable using humor? Plain and simple practice. The more you practice using humor, the more comfortable you will become. I am the prime example of a person that is not naturally funny and I know this.

However, I have worked very hard in trying to use humorous material and I'm happy to say I have become better. It required stretching on my behalf, but I consider that as a part of life. I was very uncomfortable at first, but I started to feel better and better after doing it time and time again.

2) Make sure your material is funny—There's nothing worse than using humor that only you think is funny. Not only should the material be funny to the speaker, but it must be funny to the audience.

Have you ever seen someone who really felt that his or her joke was funny and he or she was the only one laughing? One method to determine if the material is funny is to test it. You can test it on friends or strangers. It doesn't matter, just test it before using it in your speech. However, in using this technique it's imperative that the people that are being used for the test have a sense of humor.

Another way to ensure that your material is funny is to use material that you have seen other speakers use.

By all means, give credit where credit is due, though. Material that you have seen used elsewhere has already been tested. However, I must caution you, just because humor works at one location doesn't guarantee you that it'll work at another.

But, your chances are much better than using untested material. You must be mindful of the differences in the audiences.

It's helpful for you to develop the attitude that even if the audience doesn't feel that the humor is funny, you will still live through it. Speakers don't die because of bad humor. They may want to sometimes, but they don't die.

Even if you have not tested the material and you feel that your audience will appreciate it, go ahead and use it. In the event that your humor doesn't go over well, it doesn't spell disaster. There are ways to recover.

For example, you can tap on the microphone and say, "Is this on? Is this on?" Obviously, meaning that if you had heard my joke, you would be laughing. Or you may say, "I don't write them, I just say them." They get the idea. Or you can say, "Well, my mom liked it." If you remember the Tonight Show with

Johnny Carson Show, he used to follow up with cracks like that and the audience responded very well. In fact, it seemed the audience appreciated his follow-up more than his jokes. It worked for him. It'll work for you, too.

3) Use humor that relates to your topic—Regardless of how funny the material is, it should be relevant to the subject matter.

Even if your audience believes the humor is extremely funny, if it is not relevant the audience will be wondering what it has to do with the subject matter. However, if you are faced with a situation of having no humor or using humor that is unrelated to your topic, use the unrelated humor.

If you truly feel that your audience will appreciate and benefit from the humor and they will, use it. Efforts should be made to tie the humor into your presentation. This only requires a bit of creativity from you, the speaker. Most times, just one or two sentences will tie it into a related topic nicely.

4) Make sure the humor is clean—Never risk offending the audience with unclean material. People frequently ask me, "How do you define clean?" My reply always is, "You'll have to define it. Clean is *relative*." Be mindful of the event and the audience. However, I will say, if it is humor that you can use in your church, it's probably clean.

Now, in saying this in one of my seminars, I had a participant to come to me after the training session and say, "You don't know where I attend church, do you?"

5) Humor should never be offensive. Even if you think there is a remote possibility of offending some-

one, don't use it. It's not worth the risk. As in, "Have you ever heard the one about...? OOPS." It's too late, now. You can't retract it. Once it's said, it's said.

Be mindful of this. Even if you feel that only one person out of 1,000 will be offended, still do not use it. A good self-check is—if you have to stop and think about whether it will offend someone, then that should tell you to replace it with something else.

If you have to think about it, there is a good chance that it will be offensive. You don't want to take the risk. Never use humor at the expense of your audience members.

Humor is an excellent way to have your audience to love you. In the speaking business, it is said that you only need to use humor if you want to be paid.

Chapter 7

Using Visual Aids

Visual aids, if used properly, can be a great asset. However, all too often they are used incorrectly or speakers tend to rely on them too much. We all have heard that a picture is worth a thousand words. Well, a good visual aid can illustrate or prove your point much faster with fewer words.

An added bonus is your audience is much more likely to retain the information if you use visual aids. People retain:

10% of what they read
20% of what they hear
30% of what they see
50% of what they see and hear

You should use visual aids anytime you wish to: explain a complicated issue, emphasize a point, add spice, or simply to clarify. Visual aids can and should be wonderful helpers that will allow you to express your creativity and to demonstrate to the audience your depth of preparation.

Visual aids are attention-getters and can be used to create sparkle during your presentation. However, when creating and using visual aids like flip charts, overhead projectors, etc., remember the displays must be simple and neat. It's imperative that they aren't cluttered and your audience can understand them immediately. Also, speak to your audience, not to the visual aid.

Flip Charts

Flip charts are easy to use, effective and relatively inexpensive. With flip charts unlike mechanical equipment, you don't have to worry about outlets and extension cords.

Flip charts can be used in different ways. You can:

1) Prepare your material in advance. This is helpful, particularly if you are concerned about misspelling words in the presence of your audience.

I recommend this procedure for the novice speaker, primarily because if you are soliciting responses from the audience on-the-fly, you may get some unexpected feedback or you may fail to remember all of the material that you want to cover.

Sometimes in soliciting responses from the audience, some participants will deliberately suggest words that are difficult to spell. Here's a suggestion for that, if it happens to you. Simply say, "I like that. Now, spell it for me," while wearing a big smile.

Misspelling happens to experienced speakers, too. If you should ever be presented with a word that you are not sure of the spelling, remember that it doesn't and shouldn't have to be an embarrassing experience.

Here are some suggestions:
A) Ask the audience for help in spelling the word.
B) If the audience has heard what the word is, you can abbreviate it or scribble it.
C) Make a joke of it. One way is to simply say, "I have little respect for a person that can spell a word only one way."

2) Pre-write notes on flip chart. This is done by writing key words and phrases on the flip chart very

lightly with a pencil. It should be written so lightly that only you can see it and if there were someone 10 feet away from the flip chart, it wouldn't be visible to him.

This one can be extremely helpful to ensure vital information is not forgotten. The audience never has to know that the information is pre-written on the flip chart.

In using this practice, you can even maximize the effectiveness of it by appearing to think of various facts and statistics extemporaneously. Only you know that you're being helped by the pre-written notes.

This gives the impression that you truly know your subject matter. By the way this is a prime example of cheating that was discussed in Chapter 3.

3) You can tear off sheets and post them on the side of the room, if you like. This is always good to serve as a reminder to the audience in the event that you will have to refer to material from time-to-time. This activity also shows productivity and ownership by groups if there are group exercises.

I do this frequently when I'm doing seminars and there are group presentations. People like to keep their work near them. It also impresses managers when they walk into a workshop at the end of the day and are able to see how productive the session has been.

Keep the size of your group in mind when using flip charts. They are not effective for large groups. Remember, try to limit your writing to the upper two-thirds of the flip chart so the entire audience can see your print.

Avoid turning your back to your audience while discussing the content. To get pointers on this and to see it being done to perfection, watch a meteorologist on television as he gives the weather report using maps.

Handouts

Handouts are important. They allow participants to have hard copies of what's being presented and it gives them the opportunity to take notes. Additionally, it is something that the audience can keep.

One of the most common ways to distribute handouts is to simply make all of the material available to the participants at the beginning of the event or in advance.

This is problematic, however, and should be avoided, if possible. It takes care of the distribution problem and that's why most people do it, but it can and most often does create a huge distraction.

Distributing handouts in advance is generally done in a number of ways: They can be placed on the table or in the participants' seats, stuffed in registration packages, handed out at the door as participants enter the room.

The problem with this is audience members are no different from you and me; curiosity gets the best of them. They are going to thumb through ahead of you to see what's in the handout.

If, however, your presentation is such that distribution of the handouts is needed at the beginning of your presentation, then prepare a bare-bones outline with most of it blank.

That way, even if audience members get ahead of you (and they will), they will quickly realize that there is no need to do so because there is nothing to see.

However, this problem can be eliminated if material is distributed at the time it is needed. I recognize this certainly could become a problem if there are a lot of participants which means that it would be very time-consuming in distributing the handouts as you discuss them. As a speaker, you must determine the lesser of the two evils.

Things to keep in mind in providing handouts:

1) Always prepare more than you think is necessary. I have learned this one the hard way. Even if you are told an exact number, make extras anyway. It's better to be safe than sorry. Even if you don't use them all, they may be useful for other events.

I spoke with a trainer recently that told me he was presenting at an event and there were concurrent sessions. The organizer told him to have 50 copies of his handout. He made 60 instead.

Well, as it turned out, he had about 75 participants in his session. He decided that he was in a lose-lose situation. Therefore, he didn't distribute any of the handouts. I would have handled it differently.

2) Depending on the format, distribute the handouts at the time you want to discuss them—timing is everything. It may be best to distribute the handout at the conclusion of your presentation.

However, if you're going to distribute the handouts at the end, make the participants aware of this at the beginning of the presentation. It truly upsets people to learn at the conclusion of a presentation that they will be provided copies after they have taken notes tenaciously.

3) Always number your pages so the audience can follow along. By all means, make it a practice to let them know what page you are on without them having to ask. It is quite irritating to have a speaker refer-

ring to a handout when only he or she knows from what page he or she is speaking.

4) Don't put too much information in the handout. If you do, they won't read it. People like to take material away from events, but they don't like to be overloaded. The material has to readable, not intimidating.

5) Leave space so the participants can make notes. It's annoying to have material distributed to audience members only for them to discover after receiving it that there is no room for notes. People will ultimately find a place to write, but why make them hunt?

6) Three-hole punch handouts or make it accommodating for whatever type of binder the participants may be using. This shows that you really care. Additionally, the more convenient you make it for them to manage the handout, the more likely it will avoid the nearest trash can.

Overhead Projectors

Overhead projectors work well with most groups, even those with thousands of participants. I attended a seminar sometime ago with about 5,000 participants. An overhead projector was used that projected onto a giant screen. It was my first time seeing a projector used with so many people, but it worked very well.

In using overhead projectors you must be concerned about electrical outlets, extension cords, bulbs blowing and screens, walls or other surfaces for projection. Overhead projectors are easy to use; however, if you are using one for the first time be sure to find out where the on/off switch is and how to focus it before your audience arrives.

Having this knowledge up front can eliminate a potentially embarrassing situation during your presentation.

There are several rules that should be remembered when using overhead projectors. They are:

1) Test your overheads well before the audience arrives. Many of the latest models have a place for an extra bulb; make sure that it is there or carry one with you. Those bulbs are not going to last forever. There is never a convenient time for one to blow, but if you are prepared, it takes only seconds to replace.

2) Use the five lines per page, five words per line rule. Never clutter your transparency. A transparency that is too busy invites your audience to tune you out.

3) Put the overhead projector in the corner of the room. Many speakers will place the overhead projector in the center of the room. It shouldn't go there. The speaker is the main attraction.

Therefore, the speaker should be in the center of the room and the overhead projector in the corner.

4) Use sleeves or frames for transparencies. In using these, the transparencies will be kept neat and the margins can be used for helpful notes (cheat sheets). Additionally, it looks more professional.

5) Don't leave an "empty" white-light screen while you are talking. It's distracting to the audience. Bright lights automatically attract attention. This also means turning the overhead projector off between transparencies.

6) Use the revelation method. This is done by using a sheet of paper to cover the transparency and to uncover only the information that you are speaking about. Otherwise, your audience will get ahead of you if all of the information is made available for view-

ing. The revelation technique eliminates this from happening.

7) Double check for typos. They tend to stand out in an overhead. It can be quite embarrassing to discover errors at the time of your presentation. I have seen this happen countless times.

Some speakers have the audacity to say, "My assistant put this together for me and I didn't have time to check it." The audience doesn't care who put it together; they only know who's presenting it. Therefore, you will be held responsible.

8) It's always good to carry a few blank transparencies. You never know when you might need them, specifically to clarify a point.

9) Depending on the number of transparencies, you may need to number them. The magic number is five. If you have five or more the best thing to do is to number them. You never know when you might drop them. It's usually sooner, rather than later.

10) The best and most professional way to point things out on the transparency is to use a pointer on the overhead, rather than pointing to the screen. Reasons are: A) You should never turn your back to the audience; B) If you are at the overhead projector, you can still reference your notes written on the transparency frame; C) You more than likely, will not be able to point to the information located at the top of the screen.

11) Use bullets and sentence fragments. One sure way of cluttering your transparency is to write full, complete sentences.

12) Make sure the information that you are sharing is accurate and up-to-date. Inaccuracy and untimely information can destroy your credibility.

Props

Props are always good. They are the actual items or a model of the real thing. They allow you the opportunity to show the audience exactly what you are speaking about.

A good point to remember about using a prop is to reveal it only at the time you are ready to speak about it, Then remove it from the audience's view.

The reason for this is revealing it at the time you are ready to speak about it creates an air of surprise and removing it after you are done speaking about it allows the audience to return their focus to you, the speaker. If you continue to display the props after speaking about them, the audience will continue to look at them.

Video Tapes

Video tapes are very popular. It is an excellent way to illustrate a point. However, bear in mind the number of people that will be viewing it to ensure it is visible to everyone. It is a good idea to brief the audience on what to expect or to create some suspense. That way, they will be anxious to view it and be more attentive.

Here are a few points to keep in mind:

1) Check equipment well in advance. Make sure you know how to operate it prior to the audience's arrival. It's embarrassing and not a good use of your audience's time by checking it in their presence.

2) Set volume level by sitting in the last row and listening to determine how well you can hear the video. The audience doesn't appreciate a blaring video when

it's first turned on, nor should it be necessary to ask if the participants in the back can hear. If you have done your work in advance, you will know.

3) Sit in various locations around the room to ensure the screens are visible to all of your audience members. It may be necessary to angle the screen so that everyone can view it. The best way to determine this is to simply look for yourself.

4) Always cue your video. Attempting to fast-forward or rewind seems to take forever when your audience is present. Having it cued indicates to them how well-prepared you are.

5) Never show a video right after lunch. You might lose some people to the sandman. The first hour after lunch is difficult for a lot of people to stay alert and sometimes to stay awake, period. Therefore, never torture them with a video. In fact, this is really the time for something highly interactive.

High-Tech Equipment

There are many types of equipment that fall into this category. There are computers, LCD's (Liquid Crystal Display), CDI's (Compact Disk Interactive) and others. The use of high-tech equipment can be quite impressive.

There are complementing softwares to create exciting and entertaining presentations. Be mindful, however, that your entire presentation should never be completely dependent on the equipment. Things do go wrong sometimes, particularly with mechanical equipment.

I have a friend who recently told me about an incident that happened to him. He was making a presentation with a new laptop computer and the computer went to sleep on him.

He tried everything that he could to wake it, but failed. He even phoned his office to speak with the office computer guru, but he wasn't in. His presentation was "dead in the water." He said he will never forget that experience. I'm sure his audience won't forget it either.

High-tech equipment can help you create some spectacular presentations with the visual effects, sounds, etc. However, you must have a backup of some type, because the question is: when will you need it? not, *if* you will need it.

Chapter 8

Enhancing Your Speech Through Voice, Gestures And Platform Movement

What is it that makes the great speakers "great"? What is it that makes some speakers outstanding, while with others you wish their opening was their closing? Have you ever experienced a situation where you were one of several speakers at an event and people left talking about what a great job another speaker did? A speaker with content that wasn't near the quality of yours.

Do you attend meetings having done your homework and make excellent suggestions, however, you realize they are only noticed when someone else mentions them? Do you have difficulty motivating people?

All great speakers know how to maximize the use of their voice, gestures and platform movement. They understand the importance of speaking with vitality, intensity and enthusiasm. It means getting outside of yourself and fully expressing your emotions.

Initially, this may be uncomfortable, but you have to learn to step beyond your comfort zone. It doesn't mean you have to become something or some person that you are not—we all have emotions. It does mean, however, developing a part of you that may be hidden within.

Voice Quality

As a speaker, it's imperative to understand that your voice says a lot about you. It can command respect. It can also be the reason for others who had a great deal of respect for you to lose it instantly.

For example, have you ever read or heard a lot about a person and were truly impressed with him, and finally got the opportunity to meet the person? He opened his mouth to speak and immediately the sound of his voice caused you to no longer maintain those views.

When you speak, your voice is the primary link between you and your audience—it's the medium of your message. The objective is to speak with a voice that's authoritative, yet friendly. You must always have your audience members to believe that you are likeable and approachable.

I encourage my clients to record their speeches. One thing that I frequently hear is, "But, when I record it, it doesn't sound like me" as if someone else decided to do their speech for them. I have to convince them that it is their voice.

What they really mean is they are not satisfied with their voice. They are not satisfied with the way they sound, which is not unusual at all. What is unusual is for someone to say, "I don't like the way I sound and I'm going to do something about it."

Most people would prefer a voice that is deeper than their current voice—males and females. I have known this about myself for sometime now, but particularly so after being a radio talk show co-host. I would frequently play with my voice in the studio. It drove my co-hosts nuts. My favorite saying was, "Good morning and welcome to another edition of inspirations." I would always make my voice deeper than it really was, while practicing.

Middle Third

I discovered that I liked my morning voice best. It was a bit deeper than my regular voice. It had more of a resonant sound. In fact, according to Michael Hall, voice coach, professional speaker and author, the voice you hear after you first wake up is your natural "middle third" sound.

In his book *Twelve Secrets of a Great Voice* he says, "The middle third is the best sound your voice can produce. That it has the richness we enjoy hearing in a person's voice. Successful singers, broadcasters and performers use their 'Middle Third' to be more effective."

You may be wondering where is the "Middle Third." Here is how he suggests you find it. Slightly close your mouth so that your lips are barely touching. Say "Um-hum" in different pitches. Keep doing this until you feel your lips buzz. Your "Middle Third" is where you will get the most buzzing sensation.

Another quick way to check for tonality correctness is to put two fingers on the side of your throat while saying, "um-hum" in different pitches, both up and down the melodic scale.

The strong buzzing feel will be very evident to your fingers when you find the "Middle Third." Your "Middle Third" is where you will get the most projection, tonality and other sound qualities of your voice.

As a speaker, there are a number of factors to remember that can greatly affect your presentation as it relates to voice quality.

1. Vocal variety—Experienced speakers use different notes to convey variety and meaning. A monotonous speaker promotes disinterest and only invites the sandman. It's imperative to vary your voice as you speak.

This creates interest and amuses your audience. It is generally done by varying your pitch, volume and timing. Inflection is an important characteristic of speaking. This can be extremely effective in highlighting a point and adding emphasis to a word. Let's examine pitch, volume, rate of speech and pauses.

2. Pitch—The highness and lowness in the sound of your voice are known as pitch. It's very ironic that when people speak one-on-one, they quite often take advantage of this feature.

However, in speaking to groups, they tend to forget about it. It's there all the time. Learn to take advantage of it. However, I must caution you against lowering the pitch of your voice for an extended length of time.

First of all, your audience can usually tell if you are forcing the pitch of your voice down unnaturally. Secondly, it strains the throat muscles, which can cause hoarseness, laryngitis or sore throat.

3. Volume or loudness—Speakers should vary the loudness to add emphasis and greater impact to the presentation. I am always astonished to see speakers and sometimes professional speakers that do not speak loudly enough to be heard by the entire audience.

Typically, this happens when no PA (public address) system is being used. I have attended functions with speakers mumbling and someone in back yells, "Can't hear you!" The speaker then says, "Oh, I'm sorry. I'll speak louder." Even then, he does so for five minutes or so (at most) and goes right back to the same volume. It's imperative as a speaker to make sure you are being heard by your audience.

It's important to be able to maintain your volume throughout your entire sentences. Avoid becoming inaudible at the end of your sentence. This is referred to as "trailing off." This usually occurs when the speaker has used too much breath at the beginning of the sentence.

Most audiences may not make it known to you verbally that they can't hear you, but let me assure you, it is not appreciated by any audience. If you are noticing the body language of the audience, you can sense when something is going astray.

Signs of being faintly heard by the audience are: audience members start carrying on conversations with each other; people nodding off; a slow exodus by attendants in the rear; or finally people holding their hand up to their ears, gesturing that they cannot hear you.

These are from most subtle to the most obvious signs. Never give an audience a reason to tune you out. Not being able to hear the speaker is one of the more popular reasons to be tuned out.

As a speaker, though, you should be able to realize long before it gets to that point that you are not being heard. However, if you are not sure, simply ask if you are being heard. It shows that you care about your audience and the presentation. I do recommend this as a last resort only because speakers should always, as we say in the business, be able to "bounce their voice off the back wall."

Generally, when I speak of volume, I am referring

to people speaking too softly. However, speaking too loudly can also present problems. Some people have the unconscious habit of speaking too loudly.

I have a friend that has that fairly unique problem. I have never heard him speak using a PA system and quite frankly, I hope I never do. Typically, when a person is speaking too loudly or the PA system is too high, audience members will make it known right away.

Signs of the volume being too loud are hands covering the ears, or you may suddenly notice people heading for the door.

Some speakers become very skillful at whispering during their presentations. That always seems to capture the audience's attention. In using this technique, you will notice the heightened interest in your presentation indicated by audience members leaning forward with eyebrows raised.

However, you must be careful in employing this technique. It can be overdone quite easily and then you will get the same effect as not being heard by your audience. By the way, it has been said that if you whisper, people will believe you—after all, that's how rumors get started.

4. Rate of Speech—It's important that you avoid speaking too slowly or too quickly, because either tendency can distort your articulation, limit change of pitch and alter your voice quality.

A person that speaks slowly may not realize how frustrating it can be for listeners to maintain attention to what's being said. People's minds produce thoughts at a much faster rate than the flow of speech.

As aforementioned, talking too fast creates problems, too, even though, people are capable of understanding 700 to 800 words per minute. The most effective speaking rate falls within the range of 130 to 180 words per minute. You can easily keep within this range by speaking rapidly enough to avoid a boring drone, yet slowly enough to be understood.

The Use Of Pauses

Pauses are periods of silence between words and phrases. Their function is to separate ideas and hold attention. Pausing draws attention to what was previously said and when used properly, can add power and drama to your speech. It allows the audience to review your last words and reflect on how profound they were.

A brief pause can be powerful, but most important it allows you time to plan your next words. Resist the temptation to fill the space with an "uh" or "ah." These are referred to as crutch words or "fillers."

Some people have the tendency to connect "ah's" or to begin each sentence with one. They can seriously damage an otherwise good presentation. Other forms of crutch words are: so, and, well, and ya know. Speakers that do this obviously don't realize the beauty of silence.

In the radio business, I learned that silence is not appreciated. As a matter of fact, it's despised because time is money. It's referred to as "dead air." The air time must be filled. However, in speaking, take your time. Use pauses to your advantage.

Placing Emphasis

One way to add emphasis to a word is to lengthen the sound of it in your speech. For example, in saying,

"It has been a slow process" you can say, "It has been a s-l-o-w process."

In this particular case slow has been lengthened to emphasize that the process has taken a long time. Also, repetition can be effective in emphasizing a point. For example, "It has been a slow process. It-has-been-a-slow-process." It becomes quite clear that the process has been slow.

I have always been impressed with speakers that have mastered the art of speeding up during their speech and then slowing down to make a point or to place emphasis.

Gestures

Gestures are a necessary part of your presentation. Gestures are body movements that reinforce your verbal message.

Typically, when I speak of gestures, I am referring to the use of the hands and arms, but gestures can be made with the head, shoulders or even legs and feet. Some speakers even use their entire bodies for gestures.

Gestures are extremely important in being able to express yourself.

Many novice speakers are always asking themselves, "What do I do with my hands?" It's sometimes very obvious that they don't know what to do with them. "These things just get in the way," they typically say. The answer—use them for gestures. Not only can they be used for gestures, but they can be very effective visual aids for you as well.

Do not put your hands in your pockets. This is quite common, particularly for men. I always advise against that. More times than not, for men particularly, they will have coins or keys in their pockets.

Sooner or later, usually sooner, they will start to make noise with the contents of their pockets. This can be a terrible form of distraction. I have even seen people deliberately making noises with these objects. They develop rhythms with them. They don't realize how distracting it can be, but the audience surely does.

Don't hold your hands behind your back. Don't hold them in front of you—the famous fig leaf pose. For heaven's sake, don't wring them either as if they were dish towels.

Steeple Position

To convey power with the use of your hands, you should hold them in front of you in a steeple position when they are not being used for gestures. The steeple position is matching fingers together with both hands at a height just below your chest. Some even refer to it as a Christmas tree position because of its likeness.

In using gestures, don't overuse them. This is a common trait for speakers that do realize the importance of gestures, but get a bit carried away.

I have seen some speakers over-gesture, using their hands and arms as if they are engaging in karate. This too can be a distraction.

The speaker should always be mindful of how large gestures are being made. The size of one's gestures should vary depending on the size of the audience. Your goal as a speaker is to make sure that the entire audience can see your gestures, which means larger gestures for larger audiences and smaller gestures for smaller audiences.

My advice is to be mindful of your gestures, but never practice them. For example, I saw a speaker recently that obviously had been practicing his gestures. During his presentation, he came to the part that required the use of a certain gesture. He completed the sentence, then his reaction was if he suddenly realized that he was supposed to have made a gesture.

Well, rather than missing the opportunity to use the gesture, he did it anyway. The timing was off. It looked very strange for him to do it at that point. It would have been best to not use it because it was not supporting the words that were being said.

Your gestures and words should be congruent. It is truly difficult to do a presentation and try to think of each gesture that should be used to enhance your speech. The key for effective gestures is to relax as much as possible and allow your body to react naturally.

Additionally, in using gestures as a form of visual aid, you can help your audience see what you are saying. Gestures can also convey intensity as in making swift, snapping motions.

Using your fist to hit the palm of your hand to indicate shock or impact is also an effective method. Don't be afraid to pound on the lectern or podium to signify drama. This is also a way to bring your audience back into your speech.

Platform Movement

Platform Movement—changing your position or location during your speech. It can be a tremendous asset or a tremendous liability to your delivery.

Three benefits of platform movement: 1) It can support or reinforce what you say; 2) It attracts the attention of the audience; and 3) It's the fastest, most effective means of burning up nervous energy and relieving physical tension.

Our eyes are naturally drawn to moving objects. It's tedious to watch a stationary object, so you don't want to be glued to one spot while you speak, unless you're speaking at a lecture or podium with a microphone. If this is the case, then your platform movement is severely limited.

On the other hand, too much movement becomes a distraction. The novice speaker commonly rocks, sways and paces, without being aware.

Try to incorporate enough purposeful platform movement into your speeches so your body won't unconsciously indulge in distracting mannerisms. As you move about, make slow, deliberate paces.

Attire

I have purposely left attire as the last thing to discuss in this chapter. Yes—your attire can certainly enhance your speech. It can also be the reason for your audience to immediately dismiss you as a credible speaker, Right or wrong, it happens all the time.

With this in mind, it certainly would be to your advantage to dress appropriately for the occasion. Without knowing what your occasions may be, it's difficult to tell you how to dress. However, here are some pointers you should keep in mind. If you're not sure how to dress, err on the side of being dressed too formally.

If you have on a suit and realize upon arrival that it's a bit too conservative for the occasion, you can always make adjustments. On the other hand, if you attend the event with a tee shirt, jeans and sneakers, there isn't anything you can do if you realize you are too casual.

Incidentally, it's perfectly okay to inquire about the dress as you discuss issues with the meeting planner or the person that has invited you to speak. It only shows that you are a true professional.

In terms of colors, you are always interested in conveying power as a speaker. Darker colors are best for this. This would include black, navy blue and dark grey. Red is a power color for women. Men, I advise you to stay away from red, except in neckties. I will mention, however, red jackets or suits seem to work well for Sinbad and the late Jerry Clower. Please note these individuals specialize in humor.

Stay away from large plaids and bright colors such as pink, yellow, etc. Additionally, shades of brown such as beige imply naturalness, simplicity and relaxation, which is inconsistent with your mission. You want to convey power.

Avoid wearing excess makeup and jewelry. This can become a form of distraction. Do you remember Mr. T from the TV show *A-Team*? He wore lots of jewelry, right? Well, that was a part of his act. You don't want to emulate him.

Also, earrings that dangle with every movement of your head will be competing with you for your audience's attention. I saw a woman recently that had long, dangling earrings that would nearly reach her mouth when she moved her head.

During her presentation, I couldn't help wondering when they were going to hit her in the mouth.

Your attire can be an asset or a liability. As a speaker, you always want as many assets as possible.

Chapter 9

Answering Questions And Staying In Control

As a presenter, there will be presentations that will lend themselves to a question and answer session. Many people regret having to respond to questions for fear they may not know the answers, so much so, they will go over the allotted time intentionally, rather than offer a question and answer session. Then they will say, "I'll be happy to answer questions, if you will see me after the presentation. I'm afraid my time is up."

Knowing all the time that most people will not stay to ask questions. This is not a good practice.

If you truly feel that answering questions extemporaneously is not your strong point (this is a problem area for many speakers), certainly it would be beneficial to all parties to know the questions in advance.

In order to do this, you may have the participants to write their questions down beforehand for your review. By doing this, you will be able to more adequately and comfortably address their concerns.

What To Do When You Don't Know The Answer

It's important to know why people ask questions. There are various reasons: 1) Some people genuinely don't understand and need clarification; 2) Some want to draw attention to themselves or their own agenda; 3) Others want to see how much you know concerning the subject matter. Many times, you can sense the reason for the question based on how it's being asked.

Nevertheless, if you are asked a question that you don't know the answer to, admit it. Your sincerity will be appreciated by the audience. Your credibility is at stake. Don't try to bluff your way through it. Some people can do this fairly well, but many fall flat on their face.

I have two recommended ways to "save face" by not knowing the answer:

1) You can open it up to the audience by simply saying, "I don't know the answer to that, but I bet someone here does" or by saying, "Oh boy, I need some help with that one. Can anyone help me?"

In saying this, there will always be someone to stand and say, "I can help you with that one." This is an excellent one to use, because people are always willing to help. This, too, I think goes back to trying to be the teacher's pet. I have also seen this one used cleverly by the speakers simply saying, "feedback?"

2) Offer to get back to the individual with an answer. Your reply would be, "I don't know the answer to that, but I will look it up and get back to you." However, if you promise to get back to the audience member with an answer, its imperative to do so.

I have seen some people use this one and have no intentions whatsoever of getting back to the person that asked the question. If you don't know the person get their name and number or address, or better yet a business card. It isn't necessary to apologize about not having all the answers.

There are some people who simply refuse to say, "I don't know." They feel that it belittles them as a speaker. Others are reluctant to say it because they are regarded as the "expert" in their field.

If you feel for whatever reason that "I don't know" isn't an option, then you should consider these options:

1) You can give generalities in hopes of answering their questions;

2) If there is someone else at the event that is better qualified than you to answer the question, defer to him. Your reply may be, "That question deals more with John's area of expertise than mine." Then ask John for his input. However, I must caution you that it's imperative that the person that you are deferring to has the answer and doesn't mind being called on without prior notice.

Never make people feel bad or slow for asking questions. If you prefer the audience to wait until the end of your presentation to ask questions, then let them know that upfront.

This is particularly important if you feel that during the beginning of your presentation, many questions may be generated, but answers are forthcoming as your speech progresses.

Never use sarcasm when answering a question, even if you feel that the participant is asking a trick or loaded question.

Never say or do anything to make the person asking the question feel stupid. You must always have your audience feel that there are no stupid questions. In creating an open and positive environment for questions, your body language speaks louder than your words.

For example, if you say "Are there any questions?" while looking at your notes or looking down at the floor, your body language says you don't want any questions. If you are folding up your material and not looking at your audience while asking "Are there any questions?" you are less likely to get questions. If you are grabbing your keys while asking "Are there any questions," your audience will feel that you are ready to go and really don't care to address questions.

Even worse, if you put your hands on your hips, while asking if there are questions, your audience will feel that you truly don't want questions. The best way to solicit questions from your audience is to take a step toward them with your arms open and extended out to them saying, "Are there any questions?"

It's important also to pause when asking if there are questions. Many people will slow down rather than pause. It becomes quite obvious that no questions are wanted when the speaker does this. Take a four to five second pause after asking if there are questions. You can also lead your audience in asking questions in a specific area by asking, "Are there questions related to...?"

Self-Generated Questions

Have you ever wondered what to do if you open the floor up to questions and none are asked? I frequently ask this question in my seminars. The most common response I get from the audience is, "Great, be thankful and leave quickly." However, if there are no questions and you have allotted time to a question and answer period or you feel the ice must be broken, you can create questions of your own. This is referred to as self-generated questions.

One way to do this is to say, "One of the more frequent questions I get is..." After doing this, solicit questions again. If there are still no questions, you can say, "I'm often asked..." If you have done this presentation before, you will have a good feel for some of the more popular questions.

But, even if you are not, you can mention the ones that you think the audience would most likely appreciate or you may simply use the questions that you anticipated. After you have asked a few self-generated questions, you are sure to get some from the audience.

Career Day

This method really helped me during a career day that I attended some years ago. There were about 120 students with counselors and many other company representatives. I was there representing my company and I was also the guest speaker.

Many students came to my exhibit with lots of questions. I answered many of them, but asked some of the students to hold their questions until I did my presentation. They agreed. Toward the end of my presentation, I opened the floor up for questions. There was complete silence.

The kids did not utter a word. I knew, however, that there were questions. So, I said, "One of the most common questions I get is..." Still, I got no questions. Then, I said, "A question that I frequently get is..." Finally, I got my first question from a student. Once the ice was broken, I got lots of questions.

To a large degree, you can control the number of questions that the audience asks. If you have done the presentation a few times before, you will have some idea of the areas that tend to generate the most questions. You can simply make sure you cover the area thoroughly.

On the other hand, you might make plans not to address certain issues in anticipation of creating questions. Then, when the questions are asked, you appear to give a spontaneous answer. Doing this can be impressive to your audience. It's perfectly okay to do this. Even the best speakers rehearse their responses. Many cleaver politicians use this procedure, too.

Be wary of answering hypothetical questions. They tend to get a lot of speakers in trouble. Someone once said, "Only fools answer hypothetical questions."

You can also plant questions in the audience. What's meant by that is to have people to ask pre-planned questions. This is a sure way to appear well-prepared. Obviously, you will have a well-rehearsed answer when this occurs.

Repeat All Questions

As a general rule, it is always good to repeat all questions when you are making a presentation to a group.

This should be done for a number of reasons:

1) Questions should always be repeated to make sure the entire audience knows what the question is. Have you ever attended a seminar or workshop and a question was asked? However, you were sitting near the back and never heard the question. You could only hear the answer from the speaker. Irritating, wasn't it? (This is particularly important when the question is asked by someone sitting in the front of the room.)

2) Questions should always be repeated to ensure you understand the question. In repeating the question aloud, you are in essence asking the person that asked the question if you understand them correctly. You can only assure the audience member that you understand their question by repeating it. In the

event there is some misunderstanding, you can expect the audience member to clarify the question.

3) Questions should always be repeated because it gives you, the speaker, more time to prepare an answer. Time to properly formulate your answers in your own mind is critical. Regardless of how well you know the subject matter, you should take advantage of the time to formulate your thoughts and ideas in your mind prior to attempting to answer the question. You will be much more pleased with your response and so will your audience.

The three most common problems in answering questions:

1) Answering too much. Have you ever asked someone a question and he started to tell you about the history, the reason it was invented, etc.? You started to think, "Why in the world did I ask you, any-way?" The person continues to go on and on and on. You know how you feel when that happens to you. So, do not do it to others. Keep your answers brief and to the point. Long-winded answers are boring and will cause the audience to tune you out.

2) Answering too soon. Some speakers will start to answer after hearing only part of the question. They assume they know the entire question. This can also be quite embarrassing when the person that is cut off follows up saying that was not his or her question. Allow the person to finish the question. That way, you will be sure to answer the question more appropriately.

3) Avoid dialogues during your question and answer session. There are always going to be people that disagree with you. Don't allow yourself to have a dialogue with them. Offer to meet with them at the

end of your presentation or at the end of the day, if it's a full-day seminar. Then you can further discuss the issue.

Break Eye Contact

Do this in a very polite manner with a smile on your face, break eye contact and move on with your presentation. The audience will understand and appreciate your decision. It is important to have audience members feel that they were not intrusive by asking questions.

Nonetheless, it's important to understand that there are some people that like to draw attention to themselves by constantly interrupting or disagreeing with you. You should be prepared and anticipate those situations.

Never repeat a statement that is inconsistent with your position. For example, if an audience member says, "I gathered from a recent article that you are in favor of the death penalty." If in fact you are against the death penalty, you should never say, "I am in favor of the death penalty. No way." That statement is ideal for a quote out of context. A better response would be, "I am absolutely, 100 percent, against the death penalty." Then, provide information to support your position. This technique is helpful in dealing with the media as well.

Handling Troublemakers

It's important to understand that every person in every audience will not give you his undivided attention. In fact, some can be down right rude. There may be audience members that will fall asleep, have side bar conversations, walk out or even heckle you. The reasons for these actions will vary as much as the individuals that do them.

Regardless of the reasons, however, never allow an audience member to anger you. If this ever happens, you lose—they win. It is difficult to maintain a cordial and friendly facial expression if you are angry with an audience member.

Your body language will reveal it every time and it causes difficulty in performing at your very best. Even in cases when people decide to voice their opposition to your remarks, you must always take the high road.

The natural reaction is to respond in kind, but that can and usually will turn the audience against you. If you react with kindness and compassion, the audience will respect you and usually come to your defense.

If you are presenting on a subject matter that is controversial or you anticipate problems or disagreement, address it before it occurs. One way to do this is to simply say, "I realize this is a controversial issue and I know some disagree with me. However, this is my opinion or this is what my research has shown. I ask that you hear me out."

If you beat the troublemaker to the punch, it takes the sting away from his punch. It's okay for people to shake their heads in disagreement or to make disapproving facial expressions. You don't have to and should not address their behaviors.

Periodically, you will find that there are some people who are determined to throw you off track for their own personal reasons by engaging in sidebar conversations. There are several methods of dealing with these persons.

One option that works very well is to ignore them. This works well unless it's aggravating other audience members. Then, it becomes your responsibility to act. Depending on the situation, you should do the following which are listed from most subtle to most blatant:

1) Make eye contact with them maintaining a pleasant smile on your face or if it's a relatively small group and you know the person's name, use it in your speech as a positive example of some type.

If, however, no example can be worked into your presentation at the time, simply make an amusing expression or repeat a statement using their name at the end with a pleasant smile. If that doesn't work, go to option two.

2) Make eye contact with them for an extended period of time. It should amount to five seconds or more. As discussed earlier in making eye contact with your audience, if eye contact is made for longer than four seconds, it becomes uncomfortable for the audience member.

In this particular case, that is the intent. The troublemaker will get the message. However, if it doesn't work, you should move to option three.

3) Move closer to the person. While he is talking, maintain eye contact until you are standing close to him. Your physical presence (your standing right in front of him) will make him aware of his behavior and it will also draw attention to him. Once this occurs, he will stop talking.

Options four, five and six should be used with caution. Depending on the situation and person, it could cause a great deal of embarrassment for you and the audience member.

4) You can stop speaking all together (looking at the individual) and wait until the audience member ceases the disrespectful action.

5) You can ask the audience member to be quiet in

a joking manner by saying something like, "I'll be done in a few minutes. Then, it'll be your turn" or "The question and answer session will start in a few minutes." I have seen speakers say, "Is there something you would like to share with the rest of us?" This may very well get you the silence you need, but it can be quite dangerous acknowledging and allowing someone to speak to the entire group if he is already being disrespectful.

6) If your program is being disrupted to the point that you cannot go on and you have exhausted all other options, you may have to ask the person to leave. Of course, this depends on the situation and should be employed as a last resort.

There are also silent troublemakers. These are the people that don't say anything, but whose actions cause disruption. An example of this is an individual that opens a magazine or newspaper to read while you are speaking.

Another example is an individual that overtly yawns frequently. The message is meant to be quite clear, "I'm not interested in what you have to say" or "you are boring me." The best thing to do for these types of audience members is to make eye contact with them as frequently as you can with a big smile on your face.

It's important to understand that as the speaker you must maintain control. Your audience expects you to take the leadership role and will hold you responsible for the actions of others.

Tact must be used in employing any of the options outlined above. Remember, as the speaker, your audience will come to your defense if you act with compassion. I have actually had audience members to "ssshhh" people that were having sidebar conversations. I have even had them to go so far as to say to the audience member, "Be quiet."

After all, you always want the audience on your side. They will fight your battles for you, if you maintain control with compassion.

Chapter 10

Things To Avoid As A Speaker

Distractions and bad habits or mannerisms can literally destroy a good presentation. For example, you're trying to persuade your audience members to see your point of view, while staring at your notes and picking your fingernails.

It just doesn't work that way. What you do while you speak can be a liability. This chapter will deal specifically with the liabilities in the form of distractions and bad habits.

Distractions And Bad Habits

Let's discuss some of the most common distractions and bad habits:

1) Slouching.

The podium or lectern becomes a brace for the speaker. This is something that is frequently done by presenters that have gotten extremely comfortable with the audience. It's okay to relax in front of an audience, but it's imperative that you don't overdo it.

As a speaker, you must always maintain a level of professionalism, which includes good posture. By the way, good posture allows you to project your voice more freely. Bad posture prevents your breath from flowing properly and could restrict your sound.

2) Rocking or swaying from side-to-side.

This is one sure way to cause motion sickness for

your audience. Speakers that do this are very much unaware of their behavior. They are typically struggling through their speech and are focusing 100 percent on the effort.

A close kin of this distraction is shifting weight from one leg to the other. The key is to evenly balance your weight and to make slow deliberate paces when you move.

3) Rocking front-to-back.

One must be very skillful at doing this because you could easily lose your balance; however, I have seen speakers do this for an amazing amount of time. Typically, they will rock back on their heels, then rock forward on their toes. I have honestly tried this after seeing so many speakers do it. I find it difficult to do.

Every time I see a speaker do this, I'm immediately impressed with their balancing ability. So impressed, I usually can't tell you what they were talking about after their speech is concluded.

4) Prancing.

It's important to move as you speak. It's another way to maintain your audience's attention. Our eyes are naturally drawn to moving objects and light. So, it does help to move; however, too much movement becomes a major distraction. Rather than prance make slow deliberate paces as you speak.

5) Drinking beverages while speaking.

Continuous drinking can be a distraction. Sometimes, it becomes necessary for the speaker to drink due to dryness of the mouth or throat. However, it starts to cause distraction when it is done continuously. If you must drink during you presentation due to cotton mouth, then do so.

Otherwise, it's imperative to avoid drinking any-thing as you speak. I have seen speakers include a beverage as a part of their presentation. Some will even take a sip in mid-sentence. What a distraction! Never include soda, coffee, tea or any other beverage as a part of your presentation. If you must drink—water should be your choice.

6) Excessive Facial Expressions.

It is critical to use facial expressions that are con-gruent with your speech. However, it can be overdone. I have seen some speaker whom I would swear were in pain judging by their facial expressions.

Don't be caught in front of an audience looking that way. Learn to smile. It's sometimes easy to forget. So, write it or draw a happy face on your notes or cheat sheets. Remember your audience mirrors you. So, smile more.

7) Rattling keys or coins in your pocket.

I always advise my clients to keep their hands out of their pockets unless it is used for demonstration purposes. It is even more important to keep your hands out of your pockets if you have keys or coins in them.

Some speakers will entertain themselves with the noise they generate from these objects. They have no clue that it is truly irritating to the audience. If you have a history of putting your hands in your pockets unconsciously while speaking, at least remove the objects from your pocket that will cause noise.

8) Continuous use of "uhs" or "ahs."

I know many people that always start their sen-tences with "uh" or "ah" and use these many times throughout their presentation. Some people will even double or triple clutch it from time-to-time.

They have not learned to resist the temptation of using these as fillers or verbal pauses. They have not learned that silence is okay. In fact, it's much better than "uh" or "ah." As with any filler word, avoid its use. The key is to become mindful and fill that space with silence.

9) Cracking knuckles.

This is probably one of the most annoying distractions to your audience. Typically, the speakers that do this are the ones that tend to do it on a frequent basis even when they aren't speaking. It just happens naturally for them. If you must find something to do with your hands, use them for gestures.

Use the steeple technique when you aren't gesturing. As a second alternative, clench the lectern or podium. Even putting them in your pockets is better than cracking your knuckles.

10) Clicking a pen or marker.

This is something that's inevitable for me if I have a pen or marker in my hand. Therefore, when I'm done using it, I always put it away.

Otherwise, I know it's just a matter of time before I will start clicking it. Or, if it's not the clicking type, I will start pulling the cap off and putting it back on, pulling it off and putting it back on. To avoid this distraction, I simply put it away.

11) Twirling a pencil, pen or pointer.

Most speakers from time-to-time will use whatever objects that may be the most handy to point out something on an overhead projector.

May it be a pen, pencil or pointer. However, when you are finished using it, put the pencil, pen or pointer away. If you don't, sooner or later (usually sooner), you'll start playing with it.

12) Ring twisting.

If you know this is something that you frequently do, take your rings off. Be mindful, if you put them in your pocket and there are other objects in there too, they will create a jingling sound just like coins.

13) Tugging at your ear lobe.

This is usually an indication by the speaker that something isn't going as planned. Typically tugging at the ear lobe is not done throughout the speech, but is done periodically by the speaker.

In speaking with people that do this, they always reveal later that they made a mistake, forgot a part of their speech, or something unexpected occurred. There are other idiosyncrasies that may show themselves during nervous segments of your speech. Be mindful of them.

14) Adjusting glasses.

This sometimes occurs because the speaker's glasses actually need adjusting or repairing, but is also a sign of feeling uncomfortable. If in fact you find that this is happening to you because there is a need for your glasses to be adjusted or repaired, it's better to go ahead and take them off.

By the way, I have been told by some speakers that it actually helps them to take their glasses off; that way they can't see how the audience is reacting. Therefore, they are able to be more at ease while giving their presentation. However, if you are going to have difficulty seeing your notes with your glasses off, keep them on.

15) Continuously looking at one's watch.

Many times this can be the sign of a person that truly wants to adhere to the time schedule. All audiences can appreciate this. However, it becomes a distraction when it is done every minute or two. I will also add that some may feel that the speaker can't wait to get done and away from the audience.

Whatever the reason might be, here are a number of suggestions that are better than overtly watching your watch:

A) Turn your watch over so that it faces the side of your palm and casually glace at it as you make gestures with your hand.

B) Take your watch off and place it on the lectern. No one will know how frequently you view it.

C) Have someone in the audience to assist you with the time. They can alert you by using signs of some type.

D) Use a vibrating timer that straps onto your belt or waist to keep you on schedule.

16) Removing hair out of eyes.

This is a distraction that can easily be eliminated. If the hair style that you are wearing lends itself to falling in your eyes, simply pin it up or use more holding spray.

17) Twirling hair.

This usually indicates uneasiness during a speech. This distraction can easily be remedied by wearing a hair style that doesn't allow your hair to be easily accessed in that manner.

18) Stroking a beard.

This may be the reaction of a speaker that is pondering the next words or the answer to a question. Nevertheless, it causes distraction if done throughout your presentation.

19) Wringing Hands.

This is typically done when a speaker is grasping for words and frequently occurs when speaking extemporaneously. Rather than use the hands for gestures, they are being used as if they are a dishtowel.

This is also a practice that is done by speakers that experience sweaty palms. Remember, the best possible uses for your hands are gestures.

20) External Noises and Distractions.

You are asking for trouble if you are speaking in a hotel's banquet room near the kitchen. And, you are very unfortunate if you are next door to a very noisy conference. I have done a number of seminars that have a view of the swimming pool. Bad, bad idea. As a speaker, you will be competing for the participants' attention throughout the day.

Cell phones, beepers and pagers are extremely popular these days. This is happening because more and more people want to be accessible at all times. I frequently wonder how accessible one must be to carry a pager and a cell phone.

Nevertheless, most people will turn these devices off or switch them to vibrate. If they fail to do so, generally they are embarrassed if it goes off—most people. I repeat, most people are. However, it's not uncommon to have people in meetings and seminars to accept the phone call and carry on a conversation inside the room. This truly becomes disrespectful to the rest of the audience members and the speaker.

If an incident occurs that attracts the attention of most of the audience, address the situation, defuse it and move on. If you do not, you will find that you are losing a greater amount of your time by people not paying attention to you, but focusing on the incident.

10 Deadly Sins Of Public Speaking

1. Lack of preparation

There are people who like to "wing it" as they say, simply meaning, no preparation prior to speaking. It's amazing. I have actually had people tell me that they give their best speeches without preparation. Unbelievable.

Usually comments of this type indicate agony in speech preparation. I'm convinced, however, that if you think you can do well without preparing, imagine how much better you can do with practice. As I have said earlier, if you have decided to speak to an audience, then they deserve your very best. That means adequate preparation and lots of practice.

2. Reading your presentation.

Please don't do this for two reasons: It bores your audience to death and it insults their intelligence. If you are going to read your speech, just make copies of it and distribute it to the audience and they can read it at their leisure.

3. Bragging about yourself your spouse, your children, etc.

It is perfectly okay to mention any or all of the above if it is relevant to your presentation, but remember there is a fine line between informing and bragging.

4. Inappropriate humor or jokes.

We all have heard bad jokes that were not funny and very inappropriate. If you think there is a possibility that someone will be offended, leave it out!

Even if it might offend only one person out of one thousand—LEAVE IT OUT. Don't take the chance. If you have to stop and think if someone will be offended, then that is obviously the key—leave it out. Do not use humor at the expense of your audience.

5. Little eye contact.

There are some people who have a terrible time looking others in the eyes. There is no better way to connect with your audience than through eye contact. Another problem is the presenter focusing on one person or only a few people in a certain section of the audience.

If the person doesn't know you after a while you will begin to make the person feel uncomfortable and if you are focusing on a certain section of the audience, you are alienating the rest of your audience. Make eye contact with your entire audience.

6. Poor visual aids.

Many of us have heard this before, "I know you all in back can't see this, but..." Well, if you know the entire audience can't see it, don't attempt to show it to a few.

Another example is apologizing for a smeared transparency. The rule is—if you have to apologize, don't use it.

7. Distracting motions or habits.

Gestures, jingling coins in your pocket, twirling pencils or other objects. What happens is the actions compete with your message in maintaining your audience's attention.

8. Not knowing your audience.

Know to whom you are presenting in advance. It's imperative in preparing an appropriate presentation.

9. Inappropriate volume.

Speaking too softly or too loudly. Speaking too softly is much more common, particularly when no PA system is available. But there are also cases where speaking too loudly happens as well. The key is to be adequately heard by your entire audience.

10. Failure to add spice.

What I mean by spice is humor, visual aids, stories, anecdotes, etc. Wake 'em up. Entertain them, while informing or motivating them. Use spice throughout your speech.

Chapter 11

Making Knowledge Work For You

There's no doubt that your presentation skills are important to you. As evidence, you have invested the time in reading this book. However, reading this book isn't enough—as a matter of fact, it should be the beginning, rather than the end, in your attempt to improve in public speaking.

I recommend that you read this book a second time. If you didn't the first time, you should mark or highlight, in some manner, the portions that will help you the most. Utilize this book as your desktop reference. It can be quite useful as you continue to hone your skills.

A Journey

When I am asked what was my best speech? my reply is, "My next one." As I have mentioned before, good presentation skills is a journey, not a destination—you never, ever truly arrive. As long as you live, you will be able to improve upon this skill. As I see it, that's the beauty of public speaking.

After reading this book, will the nervousness associated with public speaking go away? No. Nervousness will linger as long as you are concerned about delivering a speech in a manner that is consistent with who you are.

Remember, the nervousness has to be viewed as an ally, rather than an adversary. You have got to believe that nervousness exist only to enhance your presentation.

After reading this book, will you make mistakes in future speeches? Undoubtedly, so. This book wasn't intended, nor could it ever be an instant fix-it-all in public speaking.

My hope was to arm you with knowledge (techniques and methods) that will prove to refine your public speaking skills.

Improved Self-Esteem

I only ask that you put this information to work for you and be prepared for the fruits of your labor. It will not happen in one week or one month, but over time, others will come to recognize the new you. Most importantly, you will experience daily the benefits of an improved self-esteem.

Contact Information

If you would like to order additional books or to contact Robert Little for speaking or training seminars, you may reach him at:.

Solutions Training & Development
P.O. Box 21304
Jackson, MS 39289
601.926.4375 or 1.800.489.3439
601.926.4374 Fax
E-mail: *solut2000@aol.com*
Website: www.robertlittlespeaker.com